A GUIDE TO A SENSIBLE DIVORCE

ANSWERS TO YOUR QUESTIONS

DEBORAH GRAHAM   STELLA KAVOUKIAN   ALISON ANDERSON

tellwell

Tellwell Talent
www.tellwell.ca

ISBN
978-0-2288-2677-4 (Paperback)
978-0-2288-6164-5 (eBook)

To all the families that we have worked
with and from whom we have learned so much.

TABLE OF CONTENTS

INTRODUCTION xiii

SECTION 1: FAMILY MATTERS 1

ME AND MY PARTNER 3
Should we stay together? 3
How do I tell my partner? 4
What if I am afraid of my partner? 5

TALKING WITH YOUR CHILDREN 6
How do we tell the children? 6
How do we tell them it is not their fault? 8
Should we tell the children together or separately? 8
Is there a right time to tell them? 9
Do we need to know details before we tell them? 10
What do the children need to know? 10
How do we reassure the children? 11

CHILDREN'S REACTIONS, AND PROVIDING
EMOTIONAL SUPPORT 12
What is a normal reaction? 12
What should we do after we tell them? 13
Do I need to know all the answers? 13
What if I gave an inappropriate response? 14

GRIEF 15

ADULTS AND GRIEF.. 16
How do adults grieve? 16
What if I am the only one grieving?................................ 16
How do I let go of my anger?..17
Is it okay to cry in front of the children? 17

ADULTS AND THERAPY 19
Should I get professional help?.......................................19
Should my therapist specialize in separation? 20

CHILDREN AND GRIEF...21
How do children grieve?..21
What is normal grieving? 22

HOPES FOR RECONCILIATION 23
What if my child has reconciliation fantasies?...........23
What if we are not sure if we will reconcile?...............24

CHILDREN AND THERAPY...25
How do I manage my child's behavior? 25
Do parents need to agree for child counselling?......26

PARENTING TIME AND DECISION MAKING............................27
What decisions do we need to make about children?............27
What is a parenting plan?...27
*What should we consider when discussing the
weekly schedule?* 29
How important is equal shared parenting time?................ 30
How do we determine decision-making responsibilities? 31
What if we don't have joint decision-making responsibility?...............31
*What if I don't think my partner is capable of taking care
of the children?* 32

LIVING ARRANGEMENTS 33

Should the children stay in the current home? 33

How far apart should our two homes be? 34

Should I take my child house hunting? 34

What if my partner has greater resources? 35

RELUCTANT CHILDREN 36

What if my child does not want to see their other parent? 36

What if my child does not want to see me? 37

NEW PARTNERS 38

When is it okay to introduce a new partner? 38

What are healthy boundaries? 39

SELF-CARE 40

SECTION 2: LEGAL MATTERS 41

SEPARATION, DIVORCE, AND THE AGREEMENT 42

Separation and Divorce - What's the difference? 42

The Separation Agreement – What is it? 43

Do I really need a separation agreement? 43

What if we just confirm agreements by email to each other? 44

PARENTING AND THE LAW 45

What do I need to know about the law and my children? 45

What parenting issues should be in our separation agreement? 46

SUPPORT 47

Child support – What is it and how does it work? 47

Is support payable for stepchildren? 48

*What is the difference between primary residence and
shared residence?* 48

What income is used to determine the amount payable? 49

What information do we need to provide about our incomes? 49

How long is child support paid? 49

When would the amount of child support change? 50

What about when my child goes off to post-secondary school? 50

Extraordinary expenses – What are they and how do they work? 51

What if I cannot afford an expense? 52

How will we contribute to RESPs and post-secondary expenses? ... 52

What is the best way to manage shared expenses? 53

Spousal support – What is it and how does it work? 54

Can the support be paid all at once so we have a clean break? 55

How long is spousal support paid for? 55

When would the amount of spousal support change? 56

*What if we are sure that neither one of us ever wants
spousal support?* 56

What income number do we use to calculate support? 56

What if I think my ex-partner could be working or earning more? ... 57

Life Insurance – Do I really need it and why? 57

PROPERTY DIVISION (Ontario and several other provinces) 58

What does the law saw about property division? 58

What date do we use for the property values? 59

Are there different rules for our family home? 59

What about the stuff I had when we got married? 60

How do we come up with a value for our date of marriage assets? ... 60

How do I find the value of my RRSPs when we got married? 60

*What about the home my spouse owned when we got
married and sold years ago?* 61

*Gifts and Inheritances; are they treated differently than
other assets?* 61

Common-Law versus married - Are the laws different? 62

How do we share the information about our assets and debts? 63

Notional and contingent costs - What are they? 64

THE MATRIMONIAL HOME..65

If one of us wants to buy the family home, how do we
decide what it's worth?...65
What is our furniture and other stuff worth?.............................67

PENSIONS...68

What happens with my pension?..68
Do I have to give half my pension to my spouse?.......................69

PRIVATELY OWNED BUSINESS...71

I have a business and have been told I need to value it.
Is this true, and if so, how?...71
What happens with the business we own together?....................71
The value of business is equal to the home, so should
we each keep one?...72

SECTION 3:PROCESS OPTIONS..73

Creating a separation agreement..74

What is the process for figuring this all out?.............................74
What is special about collaborative practice and mediation?.........75
What else do I need to know of collaborative practice?....................76
It sounds expensive – is it?...77
What is mediation?...77
What else do I need to know before I pick mediation?.................78
What is the same about mediation and collaborative practice?.......79
What is the difference between mediation and
collaborative practice?...79
What is traditional negotiation?...80
What is litigation and arbitration?...80
What if we want to do it ourselves?...81
Which process is right for me?..82
We decided the process, what's next?.......................................82
What do I need to do to be prepared?..83

How can I negotiate a good deal for myself? 83

Why wouldn't I want what the law says I am entitled to? 84

How do I know when to settle? 84

I want peace, but at what cost? 85

SECTION 4: THE PROFESSIONALS 87

THE LAWYER 88

Why do I need a lawyer? 88

What should I think about when hiring a lawyer? 88

When should I retain a lawyer? 89

How do I find a lawyer? 89

**THE FAMILY PROFESSIONAL, THERAPIST and
PARENTING MEDIATOR** 90

Why and when do I need a family professional? 90

What should I think about when hiring a family professional? 92

How do I find a family professional? 94

THE FINANCIAL PROFESSIONAL 95

Why and when do I need a financial professional? 95

What does a financial professional do? 96

Why don't I have my lawyer do it all for me? 98

*Why not use the accountant or financial advisor we
already have?* 98

What should I think about when hiring a financial professional? ..100

How do I find a financial professional? 101

THE MEDIATOR 103

How do I choose a mediator? 103

THE COSTS 105

How are we going to pay for the professional fees? 105

How do I keep my costs down? 105

We know what we want the agreement to say, so why spend all this money?...107

SECTION 5:ADDITIONAL INFORMATION...109

TAXES AND BENEFITS...110
How should we file taxes this year?...110
Can I get some tax breaks and social benefits as a single parent..110

HEALTH BENEFITS...112
Will I be able to stay on my ex-partner's health plan?...................112

HIGHER COSTS OF TWO HOMES...113
How are we going to manage the additional costs of running two homes?...113

RENTING VERSUS BUYING...114
I really want to own a home rather than rent. How can I do that?....114

RETIREMENT...116
I am worried about my retirement now. Will I ever be able to retire?...116

RETRAINING – GOING BACK TO WORK...117
I am going to have to go back to school. How will I afford that?......117

CONCLUSION...118
ABOUT THE AUTHORS...119

INTRODUCTION

The end of a relationship is one of life's most challenging and stressful events. In the midst of intense emotions, there are many decisions that need to be made. One of the first is the process you and your partner will use to negotiate and come to agreements. You will also need to choose professionals who are a good fit to support you at this time. You will have to make financial decisions that may have a lifelong impact on your financial well-being. If you have children, you will have to make parenting decisions as your family transitions from one home to two. All of this may seem overwhelming, but this guide provides comprehensive and pertinent information in bite-sized pieces, so that you are able to make informed decisions that consider both the here and now, as well as the future.

We would like to take a moment to introduce ourselves. Stella is a social worker, Alison is a financial planner, and Deborah is a lawyer. We are all experienced in mediation and collaborative practice. Together, we offer knowledge and insight on the emotional, financial, and legal aspects of separation and divorce. We work with people from varied backgrounds, histories, lifestyles, and situations.

Almost all of the information in this guide is applicable no matter where you live. There are some pieces of information, particularly in the legal and financial sections, that may only be applicable for those living in Canada, and once in a while we will give some legal information only applicable to those living in Ontario. These sections will be identified as "Ontario" or "Canada."

We believe that being equipped with the right information at the right time will meaningfully enhance your decision making. The format of the guide is question and answer, so you may skip around and only read the section that matters to you right now, or you might read it from cover to cover. We do not want this guide to be an overwhelming item on your to-do list; instead, it offers some helpful answers to some of the questions you may have in an approachable way.

This guide is intended for people who are wanting to work in an out-of-court system such as negotiation, mediation, or collaborative process. It provides general information and answers to some of the most frequently asked questions. Everyone has their own special circumstances, and so the information provided in this guide is a starting point. We strongly encourage you to consult with the appropriate legal, financial, or therapeutic resources. Our hope is that this guide will help you choose the professionals who are a good fit for you and allow you to make cost-effective use of their expertise.

We encourage you to put together a good team to help you through your separation and we hope that this guide supplements the information and support you receive from them. We wish you well on this challenging journey.

SECTION 1

FAMILY MATTERS

Separation is not an easy journey. Whether you have been married or partnered, a long or a short time, separation requires you to grieve the loss of your dreams, your partner, and your life as you knew it. It requires that you rearrange much of what you planned for your future. If you have children, you will have the added responsibilities of supporting your children through their grief as well as establishing a co-parenting relationship with your former partner.

The better you can take care of yourself and surround yourself with trusted supports, the more quickly you will be able to move on in your new life. One of the most important choices might be that of the professionals with whom you and your former partner will work. We will talk later about how to choose a lawyer, financial specialist, therapist or mediator.

The following are some common questions that we have been asked over the years. The responses are suggestions, not absolutes. Each person's experience differs depending on who they are, who their child is, and the specific circumstances of their situation. As such, this guide is intended to supplement the support and guidance that you receive from your separation team; it is not intended to replace it.

ME AND MY PARTNER

Discussing and deciding to separate from your partner may be a difficult and painful process, particularly if the decision is not mutual. Below are some thoughts on how to take your first steps.

Maybe we should stay together?

It is unusual for two partners to simultaneously feel equally ready to separate. Often, one person is further along than the other, rendering it that much more challenging for the person who is less motivated to separate.

Regardless, if you are experiencing significant doubts, you should take the time and effort to process with your partner, perhaps involving a mutually trusted third person or a professional. You owe it to yourself, your partner, and your children. Separation/divorce is neither an emotionally nor financially easy process.

If you are unsure of how to connect with a professional, ask your family doctor, a trusted friend, colleague, or family member. You may also contact one of your local community, social, or family-service agencies for direction. *(See more on p. 94 on How to find . . .)*

Consider your decision carefully, as well as your options.

How should I tell my partner that I would like to separate?

The issue of "the conversation" needs to start with an understanding of how your partner views your relationship and some insight into how they will likely respond. Will they be expecting the news or will they be shocked and upset? What is their investment in the relationship compared to yours? The words you choose may help set a tone for how collaboratively or combatively the initiation of a separation process may unfold. While you might feel the need to explain or justify your decision, it is important to respect that your partner might have a very different perspective on the strength, history, and challenges of your relationship. It is important not to be dismissive of their point of view. Be prepared that your partner might have a hard time hearing, accepting, or even believing your words. Helping them understand your wishes and the strength of your feelings might take several lengthy discussions and a considerable amount of time.

Be sensitive and respectful, and be prepared to hear their perspective.

I am afraid of my partner; what would be a safe way to tell them?

If you are concerned about how or when you will tell your partner because of their potential reaction, it might be wise to consult with a lawyer and/or a therapist to discuss the details of your situation prior to initiating the conversation. When you do decide to speak with your partner, it may make sense to have the conversation with a neutral third party in the room, such as a mediator or therapist, who can support both of you in the moment. If there are concerns about your partner becoming intimidating or violent, it will be important to prepare a safety plan beforehand, including having a safe place where you and potentially your children might stay if need be. Conversely, you may decide that you prefer to first find a safe place for your children and then leave the home yourself before informing your partner via letter, telephone, or a third party. Prior to doing so, it will be important to first consult with a family lawyer in order to ensure that you have a workable plan.

Take the necessary precautions to be safe by consulting with the appropriate professionals.

TALKING WITH YOUR CHILDREN

Most parents struggle with how to discuss with their children that they plan to separate from their partner. Parents dealing with their own anger, guilt, and sadness may find it difficult to maintain the supportive objectivity necessary to remain helpful to their children in managing the challenges of the days ahead. Nevertheless, parents want to get it right, mindful of the need to avoid burdening their children with their own worries and doubts.

We are very concerned about how our children will react to the news that we are separating. Any thoughts?

This is a very difficult time for all of you. The following are some general guidelines to help you approach the conversation with your children:

1. Prior to speaking with your children, you and your partner should try to establish the message that you would both like to convey. If having this conversation with your partner is too difficult, work with a mediator, therapist, or other third party to determine what you might plan to say, and how and when to deliver the message to your children.

2. You will not want to give too many details about why you are separating. After all, the decision to separate was an adult one and had nothing to do with your children. The more you involve your children in your story, the bigger the risk that they may become

embroiled in your adult affairs, which may in turn undermine their relationship with either one of you.

3. You will want to keep it simple, short, and without blame. You could say, for example, some or all of the following: "We have been having some grown-up difficulties for a while. We have tried to work on our difficulties over time, but we have not been able to manage in a way that made it okay for us. So, a decision was made to separate. This decision had nothing to do with you. It was not your fault. This will mean that you will eventually have two homes, one with each of us. We will both continue to take care of you and be there for you. We both love you very much and we will *always* love you. That part will never change."

4. If you have older children, you will want to adapt your language to make your message more age appropriate, but older kids may have specific questions or concerns that are hard to ignore. This might make you feel a personal need to either confirm or clarify the specific reasons for the separation. Be mindful that even when children ask, they do not want, nor do they need to know, all the details of why your relationship did not work out.

5. Like adults, children will process difficult information in their own unique way and at their own pace. As such, if you find your children repeatedly asking certain questions, they may simply be seeking reassurance or trying to better understand what they have heard. At these times, it is important to be supportive and consistent in your responses. As always, use your best judgement and consult with your partner before choosing to share any new information.

Keep your responses simple, do not cast blame, and use your best judgement as to what specifics you feel your child can manage. The important point is for them to know that the separation had nothing to do with them and that you will always love and take care of them.

If we tell the children that the separation was not their fault, are we not planting a seed?

If they were wondering about it, you are helping put the thought to rest, at least for the moment. If they were not wondering about it, then you are ideally reinforcing and reassuring them that they had nothing to do with the separation. Far too many children wonder if they were in some way responsible for their parents' separation. Their thoughts and beliefs are often times illogical, and they seem to string events together in ways that you would not have thought possible. For example, if they were asked to brush their teeth the previous night and refused, and then an argument ensued between the parents, they may later surmise that the reason for the separation was due to their refusal to brush their teeth. From an adult perspective, this is not logical; however, these thoughts could be very real in a child's mind.

You cannot reinforce enough that the separation was not your child's fault. Consistent reassurance will be extremely important for your child.

Should we tell the children together or separately?

When the time comes for you to tell your children, it is ideal that you and your partner tell them together. This demonstrates to your children that, despite what is happening between you and your partner, you are united in your caring attitude toward them, and that both of you want to support your children through the process. You are also ensuring that you will both be giving them the same message. If it is too difficult for you to sit together, you may also convey the news separately. The important point is to deliver the same message without denigrating or blaming the other parent, regardless of what the reasons are for your separation.

Together is ideal, if possible. If not, deliver the same message separately without denigrating or blaming the other parent to the children.

Is there a right time to tell our children?

Try to choose a date to speak with your children that is not close to another significant or special date, such as a holiday, birthday, annual event, etc. Your hope is to avoid having your child associate future special occasions with the date on which you told them about your separation.

You may also want to ensure that there are no current or upcoming stressful events, such as exams or an overnight camp. Consider telling them on a Saturday morning, so that they have the weekend to absorb the news.

Try not to ask your children to keep the separation a secret from anyone. This may create an unnecessary burden on your children. It may also cause them to think that there is something intrinsically wrong in the fact that their parents are separating.

Finally, try not to tell others before you have told your children, to ensure that they do not hear it through the grapevine.

Try to choose a date free of potential associations.

Do we need to know where we will be living, or what the weekly schedule will be before telling them that we will be separating?

You do not need to know the details of your living situation or the weekly schedule when you are telling your children that you will be separating, although some parents might prefer to know the specifics before doing so. Often parents have not worked out these practicalities in advance. If your children do ask you these types of questions before you have the specifics worked out, let them know that you do not know the details yet, but that you are working on them, and you will update them as you move along in the process. If you have worked out some details and you feel that they are ready to hear the information, you can share as much as you think they can manage in the moment without going into information overload. Regardless, make sure to let them know that they will have two loving homes and that they will always have a relationship with each of you.

Too much information can be overwhelming. Go step by step and share your knowledge and information with your children as you move forward.

My partner had an affair. I think the children should know that it isn't my fault we are separating. Is that okay?

You will want to keep your message as neutral as possible. This is not the time to air your adult issues. Your children do not want, or need, to know details. Do not get them caught in the middle by indirectly asking them to take sides. Telling your children that the other parent was having an affair or betrayed you in some other way may cause your children to feel mad at them and sorry for you. It might also be used as a justification by the other parent to denigrate you, causing an unhelpful escalation of hostility on both sides. Let your children feel free to love both of you without feeling guilty, angry, or resentful. It is one of the most generous gifts you can give your children. If you have adult children and they are asking specific questions, you will need to use your best judgment and understand your own motives for sharing additional information.

Keep the adult business between the adults. No need to involve children unnecessarily.

Will my children worry that, since we stopped loving each other, we will stop loving them as well?

Your promise is that your love for them will never change, and the love that parents have for children is very different than the love that adults have for one another. Tell your children that you will always be there for them, no matter what, and that you will do your very best to work together as two parents to create a positive atmosphere and an acceptance of each other's homes.

Show your children through your actions and words that this will never be the case.

CHILDREN'S REACTIONS, AND PROVIDING EMOTIONAL SUPPORT

Open and ongoing communication with your child is what will form and strengthen your bond, and will be the foundation of your present and future relationship with your child. Keep working with your child by asking them questions and letting them know that you are open to hearing their thoughts, worries, and fears.

How do children normally react when parents tell them that they are separating?

Each child will react differently. Some children will cry, some will go to their room and play with some toys, read, or want to be alone. Other children will say that they expected the news (whether they really did or not) and appear unsurprised, perhaps even relieved, while others might be in total shock. Be available to your child physically and emotionally during this time, but give them the space to absorb the news.

Be prepared for any reaction. Every child is different, and every reaction is acceptable.

What should we do after we have told them that we are separating?

A short time after you have spoken with your children about the separation, it is a nice idea, if possible, for both of you to hold to your commitment of being there for your children by suggesting that you do something together as a family. For example, you may want to make some popcorn and watch a movie together, eat dinner together, or go out for a hot chocolate. This will allow them to feel reassured that you are still there for them and that you are able to be supportive of one another as co-parents.

Show a united front and be supportive during this difficult time.

What if my child asks me a question and I do not know the answer?

Try not to feel pressured to answer your child's questions on the spot if you are unsure how to respond. You can say, "That's a good question. I'm not sure. Let me think about it and I'll get back to you." Take your time and reflect on the question and/or ask a friend, family member, your former partner, or therapist. Once you have a response in mind, return to your child and initiate a conversation, so that they do not feel that you were simply being dismissive. You can say, for example, "You know when you asked me 'How come you and Mom can't get along'? I was thinking about it for the last several days and I'd like to share some of my thoughts with you, if that's okay..." The fact that you are returning to your child after having reflected on the question is respectful and empowering to them.

Don't feel pressured to respond to a question immediately. Reflect upon it and return to your child with a response when you are ready.

What if I have given an inappropriate response to my child because I was angry, or I just didn't know better?

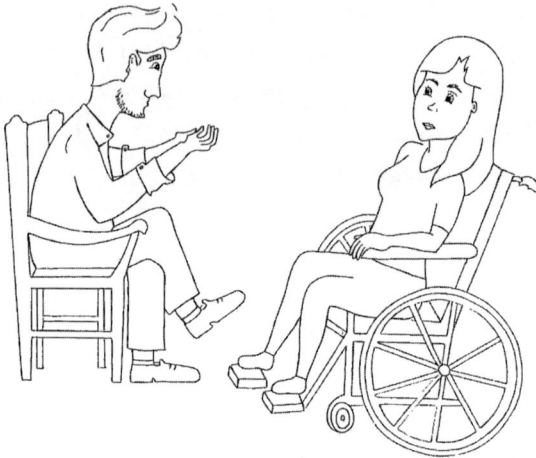

You can always return to your child a little later and say, "I was thinking about our conversation when you said that Daddy doesn't like it when we eat pizza. I know I sounded upset when I said, 'It doesn't matter what Daddy thinks.' I was reflecting that there was probably a better way for me to have responded to that. Really, what I should have said is that we each give you treats at different times and we do things in our own ways, which are not always the same way. We have our own reasons for the decisions we make. It doesn't make one better or worse than the other, they're just different. So even though we have our own approaches to things, we always try to figure out what's best for you and we both love you. I'm sorry. I shouldn't have responded in the way I did and I'm sure it didn't make you feel good. I don't always get things right, but I'm trying." This is excellent role-modelling for your child, both in terms of communication and taking ownership, and it shows that you cared enough to reflect on your conversation and returned for a different, larger conversation.

There is always room for second chances.

GRIEF

Separation and divorce are considered to be amongst the most significant stresses that people may experience during their lives. Your grieving process will vary depending on your own coping style, your level of resilience, your circumstances, and the supports available to you. This is true for both adults and children. Placing pressure on yourself or others to recover quickly will not help. Allowing time to grieve is a valuable gift to both yourself and your children.

ADULTS AND GRIEF

How do adults grieve?

There is no right or wrong way to grieve. It is an individual process. The length of time one takes to grieve varies as well. Commonly known stages of grief are denial, anger, bargaining, sadness, and acceptance.[1] Most people experience some or all of these stages/feelings, but not necessarily in this sequence. Ultimately, one's feelings of grief begin to wane over time and the intense feelings gradually lift. This does not mean that over time there may not be triggers that cause the feelings to resurface, but there should be an improved feeling of health and recovery.

Grieving is an individual process. Allow yourself the time and space to grieve.

I seem to be the only one grieving. Why is that?

Seldom are two people at the same place on the continuum of grief. This is typically because one person initiated the separation, and the other has become the surprised recipient of the news. As such, one person has been processing and grieving for a period of time before they initiated the conversation with the other. Each person is therefore at a different stage in the recovery process. The initiating person will need to allow the other

---

[1]   Reference: Elisabeth Kübler-Ross, *On Death and Dying (1969)*

person to catch up, so that together they can begin working on how to move forward. This can be frustrating for the initiating person, but it is crucial for that person to be sensitive to the other's needs. Otherwise, decisions can potentially be made in anger or spite, or for other unhelpful reasons.

Be open to receiving support as a way of managing and moving forward. Be sensitive to where the other person may be on the grief continuum.

I feel stuck. How can I let go of my anger and move forward?

People may feel angry for various reasons. Some may feel angry when relationships end because they feel wronged in how they were treated or about why the relationship ended. Others may hold on to anger as a way of maintaining a connection to their past that has been insufficiently resolved or worked through. There may also be cold comfort in hanging on to anger, as it often gives one a sense of purpose or focus. Sometimes anger may be more tolerable than feelings of sadness, emptiness, regret, or loss. Remaining in an angry place, however, can affect one's health and well-being. It can become both self-destructive and hurtful to those around us, including our children. Knowing the damage that our anger may cause might motivate us to reflect, be more self-aware, seek support, and help us to become more willing to work on ourselves in constructive ways.

Discussing and processing your feelings of sadness, betrayal, and/or anger are crucial to recovery. It will be worth it in both the short and long term.

Is it okay for me to cry in front of my children?

Grief is a normal reaction to loss, and so is becoming tearful. Separation/ divorce is a significant loss in people's lives regardless of what the relationship looked like, and how much or little the separation was seen as a welcome relief. In this regard, it is okay to be sad and even tearful in front of your children. The important point is for your children not to feel the need to take care of you or be responsible for you in the process. Let them know that you are there to take care of them, not the other way around. In addition, children tend to model their behaviour after their parents. If they see that you are not sad or grieving, they may not feel the permission to grieve themselves.

Tears are okay in private or in public!

ADULTS AND THERAPY

We live in a world that encourages us to be self-sufficient. Too often adults view the thought of seeking help, advice, or direction as evidence of personal inadequacy. People might avoid counselling out of fear, shame or embarrassment, or worry of being perceived as weak by others. It takes strength to accept that it is okay to reach out and receive support.

What would be the benefits of seeking the services of a professional when I can get support from my friends and family?

Friends and family may be a great solace and support at a time of emotional pain or hardship, but there may be times when your needs may be greater than their ability to help you. In addition, because of their lack of objectivity and/ or their desire to be supportive, family and friends may sometimes put down or blame the other partner, which will unfortunately contribute to negative feelings being promoted. A professional may be better equipped to support you during these times by providing you with the necessary guidance, advice, and strategies around how to cope with and manage your feelings.

There may also be other good reasons for you to be seeking support that are not necessarily separation/divorce related. For example, it may be that you have challenges in other areas of your life as well, such as: addictions, anger management, depression, suicidality, etc. These concerns will most likely require the support of an appropriate mental health professional.

Family and friends are important to us, but there are times when a professional is helpful and necessary.

Will it make a difference if my therapist specializes in separation/divorce?

It is preferable to ensure that the professional has experience working within the area of separation/divorce, so that they may be better equipped to understand and support you. Sometimes, therapists who do not have expertise in working with people going through a separation or divorce may err on the side of supporting their clients by simply accepting their version of events as the whole story. They may thereby inadvertently become cheerleaders for the grieving parent, acting to reinforce the very dynamics that they should be trying to minimize. Regardless of whom you choose and why, it is very important that you feel you have a good connection with that person.

Recognize when you need the extra support, identify who would be the ideal person to help you based on their experience and expertise, and ensure that you have a good connection with that person.

CHILDREN AND GRIEF

How do children grieve?

Children do not necessarily begin to grieve immediately. It could take several months for them to show signs, so it helps to stay attentive. It is typically difficult for children to tolerate long periods of sadness, so they tend to grieve in waves, surfacing for some air before dipping again, which is different from an adult's typical coping style. This is why parents may sometimes feel that their child is managing well and are then surprised to see that they are sad once again. Over time, however, the waves become smaller and more manageable.

Children grieve in waves, and over time the waves become smaller.

How can I distinguish between healthy grieving and something more worrisome?

To some degree, you are a role model for your child on how to grieve. If you provide the space and give permission for your child to cry openly and discuss their feelings, your child will most likely express some emotions. If your child has not shown any signs of grieving and more than 4–6 months have passed, you may want to consult with your child's doctor, therapist or trusted professional in order to discuss your child's emotional state. If your child appears happy and well-adjusted, however, you can simply accept that your child is managing well.

Keep your communication open and ongoing with your child so that you can have a gauge on their emotional state and well-being.

HOPES FOR RECONCILIATION

Children may fantasize about their parents reconciling. It is often their dearest hope. Remember Disney's *The Parent Trap*? In this movie, we follow the machinations of a pair of twins as they conspire to reconcile their separated parents . . . and they succeed! Try not to be surprised if your children also have a strong desire for you to reconcile. It is a normal reaction and may be part of their grieving process.

What if my child has ongoing reconciliation fantasies?

It is important for children to know that their parents' separation is final, or they can become stuck in the thought that their parents may reconcile. When this happens, they have difficulty grieving, accepting, and ultimately being able to move forward. As such, while it is vital that you are understanding of and sensitive to your children's feelings, it is also essential that you provide them with the truth. You do not need to deliver this message of finality to your children immediately, but they should be told clearly within approximately 3-6 months after you have separated that you will not be reconciling.

Support your child by not sugar-coating the reality of your situation. Speak the truth but be empathic and sensitive when delivering the news of finality. Use your best judgement as to the timing.

What if we're not sure whether we will or won't reconcile?

Many parents, like their children, will have difficulties coming to terms with their new situation and moving on. Within this context, it is helpful for each parent to have adequately addressed their own underlying doubts and any thoughts about reconciliation that may be present.

If both parents think that reconciliation might be a real possibility, they may wish to temporize or qualify their intentions to their children and frame the separation as a "trial" or as "taking a break while we work on our relationship." In most situations, however, these qualifiers are unhelpful or unnecessary, and may be confusing to your child. It is better to provide your child with some finality. If at some point in the future you do in fact reconcile, then you will have a different conversation with your children. You will explain to them that you had been working on your relationship, but that you did not tell them because you did not know where things would lead. This will be a much easier conversation to have with your children.

It is best to process your thoughts with a professional and not involve your children.

CHILDREN AND THERAPY

Often parents worry that if their child attends therapy they may feel that there is something wrong with them, or that they will be teased if their friends or peers find out. It is important that the parent frames the sessions as opportunities to think about challenges and successes in a safe and private place, and that their fears, worries, and wishes will be respected by the therapist, whom they may look upon as their own personal support person.

My child's behaviour has changed since they found out about the separation. What should I do?

Children will react and respond in a variety of ways. These may include withdrawal, isolation, crying, anger, defiance, over-compliance, etc. If you are finding that your child is behaving differently from the time prior to the separation, then the behaviour may be separation-related and you may want to seek some support for yourself (so that you can in turn support your child) and/or directly for your child. Speaking with your child's doctor or a qualified therapist will be a helpful beginning.

Seek guidance from an experienced professional such as a therapist who is ideally experienced in working with children of divorce or from your child's physician.

Does my co-parent need to agree for my child to have therapy?

The therapy will be more successful if both of you are involved. Discuss your reasons for wanting to pursue therapy for your child with your co-parent so that they can understand your concerns and rationale. If you and your co-parent have a joint decision-making agreement and you disagree on your child having therapy, you will likely require a court order to pursue therapy. Even if you have sole decision-making ability, it is still a good idea to include the co-parent in the decision, as you will want your child(ren) to feel supported in the therapy by both of their parents. There may be special circumstances, however, where it may not make sense to include your former partner. You can discuss this with the therapist in order to come to a constructive decision.

Yes, you need agreement if you have joint decision-making ability. Consider your options if you have sole decision-making ability.

PARENTING TIME AND DECISION MAKING

There are many variables to consider when making agreements with your former partner about your children. The answers are not necessarily easy to arrive at, and for some more than others it can be a difficult process. Listening to other parents claim that they have the best schedule, or that the best way to communicate with your former partner is to not communicate at all, is not going to help you determine what will make the most sense for your family. Every family has their own dynamic and every child and parent is an individual with their own specific set of circumstances to consider. One size does not fit all!

What decisions do we need to make about our children?

The most important decisions you will need to make will be related to your children's weekly schedule and your and your partner's decision-making ability. There are also several other areas that will need to be addressed when you begin working on your **parenting plan**. Much depends on who each of you are, your children, your level of conflict, your support systems, and your circumstances.

What is a parenting plan?

A parenting plan is a legal document that is a summary of all of the parents' agreements regarding their children. Parenting plans also help establish parenting principles and protocols for best practices on how to co-parent, and emphasize the importance of respectful communication between parents. It should ideally be as detailed as possible in order to avoid the potential for conflict or misunderstandings in the future. It typically addresses issues such as how parenting decisions are made with regard to medical/health/dental, education, counselling, religion, extracurricular activities, travel, and camps; a weekly schedule outlining when your children will spend time with each of you; agreements regarding who the children will be with during statutory, religious, and summer holidays, and other special occasions such as Christmas, Hanukkah, Ramadan, birthdays, Halloween etc. It also includes agreements regarding the children's official documents (e.g. passport, birth certificate, OHIP and SIN cards etc.), how to manage new partners, what will constitute a "first right of refusal," (which means that if you cannot look after your children on your scheduled time, you first need to check with the other parent if they are available before you make alternate care arrangements), how close or far apart your two homes need to be, and a dispute resolution clause so that if you have a serious dispute with your former partner, you will know what steps to follow in order to resolve it.

While there are parenting plan prototype forms and work sheets available online, it is often helpful to process the issues with a qualified social worker, psychologist, mediator, or lawyer, who can help you and your former partner create an individualized parenting plan document while keeping both of you child focused.

Parenting plans should be regarded as living documents that may require revisions over the course of time based on your children's developmental, physical and emotional needs, as well as your own changing circumstances. As such, flexibility and openness to modifications over time are critical to making your parenting plan an effective and practical document as you move forward. Your parenting plan will become a legal document when it is incorporated as part of your separation agreement. In situations where there has been a history of violence and/or a perceived or real imbalance of power, a court ordered parenting plan may become helpful and/or necessary.

What do we need to consider when figuring out our weekly parenting schedule?

It is understood that it is important for children to have healthy bonds with each of their parents. Their need to be cared for and comforted by both parents, and to have healthy communication, understanding and love are crucial to helping create the bond that enables children to grow into healthy adults. It is equally critical that parents support one another to allow them to have these much needed relationships with their children. These factors are important to consider when thinking about creating a schedule. You will also need to take into consideration your child's age, stage of development, temperament, and available supports, as well as your own personal needs and requirements. Often babies and young children will need to have more frequent contact with each of their parents and as children age they can tolerate longer stretches away from each parent. Your child's schedule may be transitional, intended to meet the needs of your child for a certain period of time, which can then transition to the next schedule, to meet your child's needs at the next developmental stage and so on, until your child has reached an age where they have outgrown the need for further modifications to the schedule.

Very long stretches, e.g., week on/week off, with perhaps a mid-week touch point with the other parent, are more often reserved for situations where there is very high conflict and/or for teenagers who prefer the stability of being in one home for a longer period of time.

Consistency, predictability, and reassurance to your child will be critical at every stage.

Consider your child's age and stage of development when creating weekly schedules.

How important is it for me to have equal shared parenting time?

The quality of a child's relationship with their parent depends more on the quality of their communication than on the amount of time they spend together. One can be living with someone full time but rarely have any meaningful conversations with them, and so the relationship becomes superficial. On the other hand, one can see one's child less frequently or have a long-distance relationship and be very connected to them through meaningful conversations. In short, a child, when growing into an adult, will rarely look back and count the number of hours or days they had with each parent. They will, however, remember the level of conflict between their parents, and the quality of their relationships with each of them. These factors will also help shape their own adult relationships and the ways they manage their own interpersonal relationships. Do what makes sense for your children, on both a practical and emotional level.

Make your decisions thoughtfully and try not to count the minutes.

How will we determine our respective decision-making responsibilities?

Decision making, as mentioned above, typically refers to medical/health/dental, education, counselling, religion, extracurricular activities, travel, and camps. If you feel that you are able to make such decisions together, then it will make sense for you to have joint decision-making ability. If, however, there are special circumstances that make it too difficult for you to make decisions together, then you may agree to have one parent responsible for certain specific decision-making areas and the co-parent responsible for the others. Alternatively, one parent may be the sole decision maker for all the relevant areas. Typically, in these instances the parent is required to consult with the other parent before making their final decision.

Try to approach this question objectively in order to assess what makes the most sense.

If we don't have a joint decision-making arrangement, what will this mean for me?

Regardless of who has sole decision-making ability, both parents can have access to all of the relevant professionals involved in their child's life. The professionals are equally obligated to keep you and your co-parent informed of your child's progress. The parent with sole decision-making authority is also typically expected to inform and consult with the other parent before final decisions are made. In general, it is encouraged that you both be engaged in your child's life. Do not stand outside where you cannot be seen or heard. Be an interested and involved parent for your child's sake.

What if I don't think my partner is capable of taking care of the children?

It is extremely important that your reasons for feeling that your former partner is not capable of taking care of the child(ren) are based on concrete information and not emotional ones. For example, it is not uncommon that parents take on differing roles during a relationship and one of you may have done more of the hands-on parenting. This does not necessarily mean that the other parent is not capable of taking on more of a parenting role in the future. If however there have been circumstances that have given you serious cause to reflect, you should take the time to speak with a lawyer, mediator, or therapist to discuss your thoughts and concerns. The professional will ask you specific questions regarding your concerns. They will ask you to critically reflect and consider whether your worries are reality-based or excessive, given your actual experiences with your former partner in the past. They will ask you for specific evidence that justifies your concerns; try to answer as honestly as possible.

If your former partner is truly unable to take care of the child(ren), your lawyer can help you decide the best path forward.

The reality is that for most families, children will benefit from a strong relationship with both parents. Having healthy, positive relationships with both parents has been shown to be an important factor in children's healthy development. In this regard, if you and your former partner are able to have a positive co-parenting relationship, you are also providing an essential model for your children by showing them that you can still work with someone even when you have meaningful differences.

Be thoughtful and objective, and seek professional advice.

LIVING ARRANGEMENTS

Our home is a material possession, but over time it may come to represent much more to us than just the four walls that surround us. For some, our homes are filled with fond memories and provide us with comfort and security. Our children may also have a strong attachment to their home. We can consequently get charged up about the decisions we need to make about our homes.

Is it important for the children to remain in the current home?

It is not necessary, but it may be helpful. Typically, most people will not have the financial means to entertain such an idea. If one of you can afford to remain in the current home for a short period of time, then it will provide some additional stability to your children's lives. If not, do not worry, your children will understand. You will create a new home with them with a new beginning and narrative. If you will be selling the home, a way of providing them with some closure is to offer them the opportunity to make a scrapbook, take photos, or create a video-recording of the home, and keep memories alive by recounting stories.

Do what makes the most practical and economic sense for you.

How far apart should our two homes be? Does it matter?

Moving to a new community that your child is unfamiliar with and that requires them to find new friends, relocate to a new school, and develop new extracurricular activities will mean additional challenges to their adjustment. If the two parental homes are far apart, it can also become difficult for children to go back and forth between them. Older children may resist spending time with a parent if they live outside of the community where the child goes to school or where most of their friends live. Whenever possible, try to purchase or rent your new homes closer to one another and/ or the school that the children are attending. Sometimes, however, due to financial and other considerations there may be little choice.

Ideally it would be best for your two homes to be closer to each other and if possible, for your children to remain in their neighbourhood or community.

Should I bring my child along when I am looking for a new home?

You do not need to bring your child along until you have found a home that you are seriously considering or have decided upon. At that point, you can let them know that you have seen a house/apartment you are thinking may be a good fit for all of you and that you would like them to see it too. You can have the children progressively become acquainted with the new home by first driving by, then walking through it on a few occasions. Having the other parent tour the home with the children may be supportive and comforting to the children. You might ask your child if they have any decorative preferences such as paint colours, pictures, or drapes for their bedroom. If you will be purchasing new furniture, you can take them shopping with you and ask them for their opinion. This will allow them to feel that they have some ownership and control.

Include your children in the decision making as a way of helping them feel included and empowered.

My co-parent is going to have a much nicer home and lifestyle than me. What impact will this have on my relationship with my children?

Children do not typically enjoy being with one or the other parent due merely to economic reasons. Contrary to what we may think, children are not by nature very materialistic. They are just as happy to sit and play a board game, make a snowman, go to the park, or read a book as they are to go swimming at a beach. For them, it is the time spent with their parent that ultimately matters. If they do have the chance to go on a vacation it will only add to their life experience, as will painting on a canvas in a nearby park. Similarly, the physical area of a house is simply a space. It is the people in the house that make it meaningful or not.

Remember, bigger is not better . . . and don't let your children think so either!

RELUCTANT CHILDREN

It is generally considered to be in children's best interests to have a good, healthy relationship with both of their parents. Exceptions are when the court has found that the children should only be seeing a parent under limited or supervised conditions, or that the children should not be seeing that parent at all. Otherwise, encourage, support, and promote your child's relationship with the other parent.

My children are saying that they do not want to have anything to do with their father/mother. What should I do?

As parents, particularly when in a situation of conflict with a former partner, we may sometimes become so passionate about our point of view that we do not always clearly know the best path to pursue. We want to protect our children at whatever cost. Sometimes, however, it is hard to decipher whose needs we are serving.

Children do not necessarily know what is in their own best interests, and we do not want to unnecessarily burden them with these kinds of decisions or empower them in unhealthy ways. They may become caught up in conflicting interests and feel the need to side with one parent over the other due to feelings of guilt, remorse, anger, sadness, or a sense of betrayal. Often, it is very helpful to be direct and firm with your child in telling them that they need to see their other parent and that it is not a choice.

On the other hand, they may have had negative experiences with that parent that are grounded in reality. Children can and should provide their thoughts and feelings when appropriate, but we must combine their opinions with the perspectives of more experienced adults and professionals, who have enough objectivity and emotional distance from the conflict to consider the child's long-term interests and needs. If there is a genuine desire to listen and address the children's needs by everyone involved (parents, lawyers, therapists, judges), the chances are optimized for a successful outcome.

What if my child does not want to see me?

Legitimately reflect on what your child's concerns and feelings are and try to address them genuinely. Try to keep connected with your child through various channels. If possible, ask for your former partner's support. Discuss with your former partner whether temporarily modifying the weekly schedule to meet your child's needs would be helpful. If your child is becoming more and more resistant to seeing you, it will be helpful to seek professional support.

NEW PARTNERS

When is it okay to introduce a new partner to the children?

This can be a sensitive topic for many parents. Aside from being extremely mindful as to how the other parent may be feeling, there is usually a golden rule regarding new partners: neither parent should introduce a new partner to the children unless they consider that individual to be a true significant other in their life. The idea here is that you are trying to minimize losses and uncertainty for your child by not introducing people who they may bond with, only to lose that person from their life if the adult relationship does not work out.

If the parent feels that the individual will be a significant person in their life and they would like to introduce that person to the children, they should inform the other parent of their intentions before any introductions are made. One of the reasons for first telling your former partner of your plans is not because they have veto power over your decision, but because it is better for your children if they are not the ones to give their parent that news. Parents tend to handle this news better if they are not blindsided and have time to deal with their own feelings about it first.

Normally, parents will agree upon a time period during which neither of them will make any introductions to the children. This period will often commence from the time when parents physically stop living together. The idea is to allow the children the time to grieve without introducing new elements into the mix.

Be sensitive to and respectful of your child and the other parent when considering the possibility of introducing a new partner.

What are healthy boundaries?

Sometimes having a new partner may evoke a reaction from your former partner. Ensure that you are not involving yourself in issues unnecessarily. In general, if your former partner is sending you unproductive emails; leaving you long, unhelpful, or abusive voice messages, or trying to engage you in unconstructive dialogue, do not feel obligated to respond. Be sufficiently self-aware so that you can identify what may be triggering to you and avoid those situations. Likewise, try not to engage in behaviour that can be triggering to the other parent. In the end, it is your child who will be the most impacted.

Try to pick your battles and don't personalize issues which are not yours to own.

SELF-CARE

It is important to look after our emotional and physical needs during times of stress. We need to be aware of the impact that our personal lives, work, and environment have on us. Knowing how to identify possible triggers and developing constructive coping responses is an excellent start. Eliminate negative habits and patterns. Reach out for support from friends, family, and professionals.

Finding time in your busy lives is difficult, especially as a single parent. Carving out specific "me time" and sticking to them has a positive effect on your general well-being. For example, swap babysitting with a friend so that you can both have some "me time", buy a DVD or an exercise/fitness app, take your kids with you for a walk or a run, write in a journal, have quiet time or shop, and eat healthily without depriving yourself. Sharing your plan with others may help reinforce your commitment to your goals. And don't forget to spend some time with your friends.

Taking care of ourselves helps us take care of our children.

SECTION 2

LEGAL MATTERS

There are various laws that come into play when a couple separates. Wherever you live will have laws relating to how you will make decisions about your children, when they will spend time with each parent, whether one spouse will pay some kind of financial support to the other, and how the assets and debts will be divided. In Canada, some of these laws are provincial and vary from province to province. Some are federal and are consistent across the country. Some laws are set out in various pieces of legislation and some are developed by the courts. Some laws only apply to separating couples who are married, and some others apply to those who were living common law.

It is critically important that you consult with a lawyer to understand the laws as they relate to your very specific and unique situation. The internet, nor this or any guide is a substitute for customized legal information provided by a lawyer who focuses on family law in your jurisdiction.

In this guide, we have provided some very general high-level principles to prepare you for meetings with your lawyer and to supplement and reinforce the information that they provide to you.

SEPARATION, DIVORCE, AND THE AGREEMENT

Separation and divorce – what's the difference?

The words "divorce" and "separation" are often used as synonyms in everyday conversation; however, they are legally distinct.

In Canada, you are considered separated when you or your former partner declares the marriage to be over and you begin to do things differently as a result (e.g., hire lawyers, see a parenting mediator, tell your families about the separation, stop showing up in the world as a couple, living in separate homes). For Canada Revenue Agency's (CRA) purposes, they consider you separated only after you have been living in separate residences for 90 days. You do not need a court order to say you are separated.

Divorce, on the other hand, must be granted by a judge. Divorce ends the legal relationship created by marriage and allows you to remarry. In Canada, you may apply for a divorce after you and your former partner have been separated for one year.

Marriage requires a decision by two people. Separation requires a decision by only one person. Divorce requires the decision of a judge.

The separation agreement – what is it?

Your separation will require you and your former partner to resolve issues, which typically include parenting, property division, and financial support. The separation agreement will set out the terms and agreements that the two of you reach on these issues and often includes three categories of rights and responsibilities. Firstly, if there are children of the relationship you need to decide how parenting time and parenting decisions will be shared between you. Secondly, you need to determine whether child support and/or spousal support are payable, and if so how much and for how long. And thirdly, you and your partner need to decide how to share the value of the net worth accumulated during the marriage or the relationship.

Do I really need a separation agreement?

It is best to have the agreements you and your former partner have reached confirmed in writing. A separation agreement sets out all the conditions so that if anyone forgets or changes their mind, there is a written document that captured what was agreed to. Sometimes, by writing down the agreements reached, we realize there is not as much clarity as we thought, and it is an opportunity to get specific and confirm exactly what is and is not agreed to. Finally, it creates peace of mind knowing that these matters are settled.

The separation agreement is also a roadmap setting out when things need to change and the process for changing them. For example, it might say that the financial arrangements need to change when the children go to university and that you and your former partner will go to mediation to figure out what the new arrangements should be.

What if we just confirm our agreements by email to each other?

For an agreement between former spouses to be binding it must be in writing, signed and witnessed. An email exchange does not meet these requirements.

There are two additional requirements: full and accurate financial disclosure and an understanding by both of you of what the agreement says and its implications. This last requirement is best met by each of you reviewing the agreement with a lawyer before signing it.

PARENTING AND THE LAW

What do I need to know about the law and my children?

You and your former partner will need to figure out when your children will be living or spending time with each of you during the regular school year and holidays.

The parenting schedule may be a primary, shared, or split-residency schedule. With shared parenting, children will spend nearly equal time with each parent. In primary parenting, the child lives primarily with one parent but will almost always have time with the other; for example: on alternate weekends and one evening each week. In split parenting, one child would live with one parent and the second child would live with the other.

You and your former partner also need to figure out how you will make decisions about education, health, religion, and extracurricular activities. In Canada, this is called "decision-making responsibility" (formerly called "custody"). You and the other parent will need to decide if you will make decisions relating to these four areas together, if each parent will be responsible for different areas, or if only one of you will have the right to decide.

What parenting issues should be in our separation agreement?

At a minimum, every separation agreement should include a parenting schedule so everyone knows when the children will be with each parent during both the regular school year and on holidays. In addition, it should include how you and your co-parent will make decisions relating to education, health, religion, and extracurricular activities and what process you will use if you disagree. And finally, it should include some specifics around how far either of you can move before the parenting plan needs to be reviewed or revised.

A separation agreement should include a parenting schedule of when the children will be with each parent, and it should set out whether parenting decisions need to be agreed upon or if they will be made by one parent.

SUPPORT

Support is where one partner pays the other partner an amount of money, usually on a monthly basis. There are two different types of support: one is called "child support" and the other is called "spousal support."

Child support (Canada) - what is it and how does it work?

Child support is intended to help a parent with the day-to-day expenses of the children, which typically include food, shelter, and clothing. The recipient parent does not need to account for how the money is spent. For most families, child support is very straightforward due to the existence of the Federal Child Support Guidelines, which have an amount, often called the "table amount," set out for different incomes and number of children. The Federal Child Support Guidelines can be found online.

The parent paying the child support is typically called the payor and child support is a monthly payment that is based on the payor's income, the number of children, the payor's province of residence, and the parenting arrangements. The monthly amount of child support is not taxable income for the recipient and is paid with after-tax dollars by the payor.

In a primary residence schedule (where the children live mostly with one parent), only one parent would pay child support. In a shared parenting situation, each parent would pay the other parent a child support amount based on the same guidelines, and the net difference between these amounts is called a "set-off." For example, if one parent's obligation was $600 per month and the other parent had to pay $200 per month. the net set-off amount would be $400 per month.

Is support payable for stepchildren?

Parents are obligated to support biological and adoptive children. Sometimes, a stepparent can be required to continue supporting a stepchild after the breakdown of the relationship with the child's parent.

What is the difference between primary residence and shared residence?

Primary residence is defined as the children living with one parent more than 60 percent of the time. There are many ways to calculate time to determine whether this threshold has been passed, such as whether sleeping time or school time are considered or not.

Whether parenting is considered primary or shared can impact the child support under the legal model.

For example, a parent having less than 40 percent of the time will pay the full table amount of child support to the other parent, whereas a parent having more than 40 percent of the time may pay a set-off amount with a possible adjustment, depending on several factors.

Where possible, it is helpful for parents to work out parenting arrangements that are in the best interest of the children regardless of the percentages of time, and then to work out financial arrangements in a way that makes sense and ensures that both parents are okay, and that the children have a reasonably similar standard of living in each household.

What income is used to determine the amount payable?

Child support is based on income from all sources, so it includes things like your base salary, employee benefits (e.g. a car allowance), bonuses, other forms of executive compensation, overtime pay, rental income, and any investment income. In simple terms, all income that appears above line 15000 on your tax return is the starting point for calculating child support.

What information do we need to provide about our incomes?

You will need to exchange information on all sources of income, and this usually means providing income tax returns, notices of assessment or re-assessment, current and end-of-year paystubs, and employment contracts. For someone who is self-employed, the disclosure needs to include financial information for the business and corporate tax returns if it is incorporated.

How long is child support paid?

Child support typically ends when a child finishes their education. If a child graduates from high school, turns 18, and doesn't go on to university or college, then child support will likely end for that child. For those children who go on to post-secondary education, child support will likely continue until they complete their first degree or diploma.

Many children need some time to find employment after graduating, so you and the other parent may choose to have support continue for some period to allow for time to transition.

Child support may continue longer for children who have disabilities that impact their ability to support themselves.

When would the amount of child support change?

The amount of child support is usually adjusted every year to reflect the previous year's incomes. It is also adjusted if something major changes, such as a job loss or significant promotion. Finally, it will also be affected if the parenting arrangements change.

What about when my child goes off to post-secondary school?

When a child is attending a post-secondary education program and is living away from home, typically the child support is reduced for that child to what is sometimes called the "summer formula." This is a reduced amount of support to reflect that the child is living away at school with parents paying for food and accommodation during those 8 months, and covering expenses for the 4 months the child is back at home. It also reflects the fact that parents still need to maintain adequate accommodation when the child comes home.

Child support is a monthly payment from one parent to the other based on incomes and parenting arrangements.

Extraordinary expenses (Canada) – what are they and how do they work?

In addition to the day-to-day expenses like food, shelter, and clothing, there may be other expenses that are considered special and extraordinary (sometimes called "Section 7 expenses"). These special and extraordinary expenses are not expected to be covered with basic child support and are often shared between parents proportionate to their income. Typically, these expenses would include childcare and camp costs, dental and orthodontic expenses, counselling, medical expenses, and many types of extracurricular activities.

For extracurricular activities, what is considered a shareable expense differs depending on the income of the parents and the amount of the monthly child-support payment.

What if I cannot afford an expense?

If your children did not have an extracurricular activity or other expenses such as private school prior to the separation, then you and your co-parent would have to agree before the expense is undertaken. On the other hand, if the children have been doing an activity for a while, such as piano lessons, it will be expected that they continue with that activity. Having said that, with the additional expenses of two households there may be some expenses that need to be cut back on, and that may include some of the expenses relating to the children.

How will we contribute to RESPs and post-secondary expenses?

If you have Registered Education Savings Plans for your children now, your separation agreement should include what you have agreed upon for how those funds will be used. Most often, any funds removed from the plan when your child is attending post-secondary school will be applied to the agreed-upon expenses prior to any sharing of the remaining costs.

The opportunity to contribute to the RESP and receive a government grant exists up to and including the year a child turns 17 if you have contributed something prior to age 16. You will need to come to an agreement about how you will use the remaining contribution room. If your children are young and post-secondary school is a long way off, it is often best for each of you to open new accounts in your own name and no longer have any contributions within the joint RESP account. The joint RESP account would be left to grow until you both agree to access it.

The good news for residents of Ontario is that, because you are separated, your children will very likely qualify for more assistance from the Ontario Student Assistance Program (OSAP) than they otherwise would have if you were not separated. OSAP provides loans and grants to qualifying students, and the loans are interest-free until the student is finished their degree. Loan repayment begins after graduation, and sooner if the child has stopped attending school.

There are student assistance programs in all provinces and territories across Canada and we recommend you contact them to find out what aid is available to your child.

What is the best way to manage shared expenses?

The solution for your family will depend on how much interaction and trust there is between you and the other parent. Usually, parents will come to an agreement on what the expenses associated with the children are and then a way to manage them.

Some common management approaches are:

1.   One parent pays for all expenses and the other parent pays a monthly amount to that parent to cover their share.

2. A joint bank account or credit card to be used solely for child expenses. This provides transparency but it does require trust that you will both be responsible in your spending.

3. Each pays whatever expenses there are when they have the children and then does a reconciliation on a monthly, quarterly, or yearly basis.

4. One parent pays all the section 7 expenses and the other parent reimburses their share at the time of the expense, or each pays their portion directly.

There are some extra expenses that are not expected to be covered by the monthly child support amount, and these agreed-upon extra expenses are usually shared proportionate to the parents respective incomes.

Spousal support (Canada) – what is it and how does it work?

In some circumstances, you or your former partner may have to pay spousal support to the other. It is not automatic like child support and can be one of the more complicated areas of family law.

The first step is to determine whether the lower-income person has an entitlement to receive support. The length of your marriage and cohabitation, the roles assumed during your relationship, the parenting responsibilities before and after separation, the extent of the disparity between incomes, and the ages of the spouses are all relevant to determine if spousal support ought to be paid, and if so, how much and for how long. Once entitlement has been established, there are Spousal Support Advisory Guidelines (SSAGs) which help determine the amount and duration.

Spousal support is typically paid monthly and is tax deductible for the payor and taxable for the recipient. Often the payor is in a higher tax bracket than the recipient, and this results in a tax savings where the combined after-tax family income is greater than it was when you were living together. This tax savings can help to offset the additional costs associated with separation, the main one being the cost of an additional residence.

In some circumstances, the payor's income may be extremely high and the range of support amounts in the SSAG is not as helpful to determine the right amount of support.

Can the support be paid all at once so we have a clean break?

You and your former partner may wish to deal with spousal support as a lump-sum one-time payment rather than on an ongoing monthly basis. There will be no tax savings with a lump-sum payment and the approach often brings an end to the spousal support obligation. Despite the loss of tax savings, there may be many cases where lump-sum support makes sense. A lump-sum approach requires both of you to consider all the possible things that might happen in the future, such as promotions, job losses, re-partnering, illness, disability, etc. The lump sum achieves finality, so you both must be willing to live with it even if life turns out differently than anticipated. It doesn't allow for things to change when circumstances change.

A hybrid version of the two models would involve a partial lump sum and a smaller monthly amount.

The reality is that many are not able to pay a lump sum and still be able achieve their lifestyle goals.

How long is spousal support paid for?

Spousal support is sometimes "time-limited," meaning there is a specific end date in place. Other times it is "indefinite," meaning that there is no particular end date set, but that when things change the support may end. Don't panic if you are the payor and you hear the term "indefinite," since it rarely means forever. It just means that it is hard to know now when it should end. When support is indefinite, it often ends up being paid until the payor retires, assuming that the retirement occurs at a reasonable age.

When would the amount of spousal support change?

Typically, spousal support is not adjusted every year the way child support is. It is only adjusted if something significant changes, which is referred to as a "material change." Common examples of a material change include a loss of job, a significant change of income for either person, the recipient of support remarrying or living with someone for a significant period of time, or children transitioning to post-secondary school or becoming independent.

Spousal support is a complex area of law, making it particularly important to consult with a lawyer.

What if we are sure that neither one of us ever wants spousal support?

You may want to consider what is called a "release" of spousal support, which creates finality and certainty. It means that even if something catastrophic happens in the future, it would not allow you to receive spousal support, nor would you be required to pay it.

What income number do we use to calculate support?

Spousal support is based on your total employment income, which includes bonuses and other types of variable compensation as well as taxable benefits like a car allowance. It can also include income from investments and rental properties.

If you and your former partner have employment income where you receive a T4 each year, calculating support is usually very straightforward.

If you or your former partner are self-employed or able to deduct employment expenses for tax purposes, certain steps are required to determine what income amount should be used as a basis for determining support.

What if I think my ex-partner could be working or earning more?

One of you might be unemployed or working only part time, and this can sometimes trigger an imputation of income. Imputing income involves using an income for what someone *could* be earning in accordance with their education and work experience. This is both a complicated legal issue and a complicated negotiation issue, especially if it is connected to some of the reasons the relationship ended in the first place, so be sure to speak to your lawyer if you are concerned about this.

Spousal support is paid in certain circumstances. The amount and duration are based on incomes, length of the cohabitation or marriage, and ages.

Life insurance – do I really need it, and why?

If either person has a support obligation, whether child or spousal, they will need to purchase some sort of insurance to ensure that, in the event of their passing away prior to the end of those obligations, there are funds available to pay out the remaining amounts. Many people who don't already have insurance in place wonder why they can't just designate a portion of their estate in their will. The reason is that a will can always be changed, and even if it is not, the funds may not be immediately available to the other person for many reasons associated with settling an estate. With insurance, the recipient can be named as an irrevocable beneficiary, which means that as long as the policy is in place they cannot be removed without their consent.

PROPERTY DIVISION (Ontario and several other provinces)

Property division is an area of law that is dealt with on a provincial basis. In Ontario, the rules differ according to whether you are married versus living together in a common-law relationship. When we refer to "property," it means all your assets and debts, not only real estate property.

What does the law say about property division?

If you are a married couple, the property rules that apply to you are called "Equalization of Net Family Property." The basic premise is that the change in net worth that occurred during the marriage is shared. There are very specific rules around how this is calculated. Start with calculating the net worth for each of you on the date of separation. Then subtract the net worth you each had on the date of marriage. These are called "deductions." Next subtract certain gifts or inheritances that either of you may have received during the marriage if they comply with defined tracing rules. These are called "exclusions." The result of this calculation for each of you is called your "Net Family Property." In order to equalize, the spouse who has the higher value will owe half the difference to their spouse, which is called an "equalization payment."

What date do we use for property values?

You would use the date of separation as the date to value your respective assets and debts. While separation feels like a process to many couples, the law defines it as a particular day. It is the date that you or your former partner told the other that the marriage was over and there were no further mutual efforts to work on the marriage or reconciliation. In addition, you and your spouse must have begun to do things differently that indicate to those around you that you are separated. Finally, you must be living separately. There has been a broad interpretation of the concept of living separate and apart, and it can include you and your former partner living in the same house but doing things a bit differently. For example, it may mean that you have told your friends, family or children that you are separating. It may mean that you have hired lawyers to help negotiate a separation agreement. The official date of separation is called the "valuation date." Sometimes it is clear and easy to determine; sometimes it is more complicated.

Are there different rules for our family home?

The family home and any vacation properties (e.g. cottage) in which you and your spouse were living in or spending time at when you separated are called "matrimonial homes." They are sometimes treated differently than other property.

One example of this is that both you and your former partner have the right to stay in the home even after separation, regardless of which of you own the home.

Another example is that if one of you came into the marriage with a home or cottage which is still a matrimonial home (meaning you and your family live in or use it as a family vacation property) at the date of separation, you are no longer able to claim the value of the home on the date of marriage as a deduction for the purposes of the equalization of net family property.

Finally, if you received a gift or inheritance that you invested in a matrimonial home, you are no longer able to exclude the value of that inheritance.

What about the stuff I had when we got married?

You or your spouse may get what is called a "Date of Marriage Deduction" that allows you to subtract the value of those assets on the marriage date (or add the value of the debt) before determining the value that needs to be equalized. You do not need to own these assets when you separate, and it is only the value of the asset on the day that you married that you get to deduct. If you still have that asset, or you sold it after marriage for an amount that was greater than the date-of-marriage value, it is still only the date-of-marriage value that you get to deduct. Any increase or decrease in the value is shared with your spouse.

How do we come up with a value for our date of marriage assets?

The legal rule is that the person who is asserting a deduction for a date-of-marriage asset must provide documentation to prove it. You might decide to take a "good enough" approach, with you and your ex-partner agreeing on a value for your respective assets and debts that accords with your recollections. They may or may not be loosely supported by some documentation.

How do I find the value of my RRSPs we got married?

The banks and investment companies generally do not keep records after 7 years, but you could start with reaching out to them to see what they might be able to find. You could log in to "My Account" on the Canada Revenue Agency (CRA) website and go to the RRSP area where you can find your contribution history by year. This is a good starting point for coming up with a value.

My Account is an electronic service that lets individuals see the details of their tax files. After setting up your account, it will take a few weeks to get an authorization code in the mail from CRA before you can access any information. This is an added level of security that CRA uses to ensure that not just anybody can access your information.

What about the home my spouse had when we got married and sold years ago?

With real estate property, unless you sold it right at the time you married, you will have to look at options for determining a value on the date you married that is agreeable to you both. It is not just the value you sold it for, because you are only able to deduct its value at the date of marriage; any increase or decrease in value after the marriage is shared.

One approach may be to prorate the increase or decrease in the same proportions as the periods owned before and after marriage. Another may be to use historical market information and assign the gain or loss to the respective periods in a way that mirrors the market. Some people opt to hire an appraiser to provide an opinion of value.

Gifts and inheritances: are they treated differently than other assets?

If you alone, or your spouse alone, received a gift or inheritance from a third party during the marriage, that asset will usually be excluded from property division, as long as you still have that asset on the date of separation and it has not been invested into the family home or mingled with other family assets. Tracing rules are complicated, and this is an area to speak to your lawyer about.

Common law versus married: are the laws different? (Canada)

If you have been living together but are not married, there is an entirely different set of principles and rules for the division of property in Canada.

The first presumption is that you don't need to share the value of it with your former partner, nor do you receive a share of their assets. Unlike the legislation for married people which creates a calculation to share the change in net worth during the marriage, there are no hard and fast sharing rules or calculation for non-married couples.

Since our legislation did not create property division rules for people who are not married, the courts have developed complicated legal concepts of constructive trust, resulting trust, and joint family ventures for dividing property to address unfair or inequitable outcomes.

Recently, the Supreme Court of Canada created a concept called "Joint Family Venture." In order to determine whether a common-law couple has a Joint Family Venture, there are four categories that are explored and evaluated: intentions, how integrated the couple's finances were, whether they raised a family together, and how much effort was shared raising the family and/or acquiring assets.

If it is determined that there is a Joint Family Venture, the value of some assets may be shared.

Also, there is no special status for the home, because without a marriage there is no matrimonial home.

This is a complex and developing area of family law that is very dependent on facts, so if you think this applies to your relationship, ask your lawyer about it.

How do we share the information about our assets and debts?

Thorough financial disclosure is a key component in making sure you and your former spouse are making fully informed decisions. It also helps to make sure that your separation agreement is durable and won't be questioned or overturned one day due to a lack of financial disclosure.

The most common way to begin the negotiation process to create a financial resolution is financial disclosure, and involves supplying your lawyer or financial professional with all the information related to the assets that you owned and the debts that you owed on the date of separation. If you are married, you will need the same information for the date of marriage as well as any property that you may have received as a gift or inheritance during the marriage. If you were living common law, it may also be important to provide information on your assets and debts from the date you began living together.

Often this is as easy as getting your bank account or investment statements and your credit card and mortgage statements. On the other hand, it can be more complicated, as in the case of a privately owned business, stock options, and the tax implications on various assets. There are professionals who can be hired to help you and your spouse determine the value of the more complicated assets and debts.

All items need to include supporting documentation that provides details of the asset or debt and its value on the separation date. You will also need to provide current information on your income as well as full tax returns for the last three years.

Unless they signed a contract opting out, each spouse is entitled to share in the increase (or decrease) in the value associated with the marriage. This is called "Equalization of Net Family Property."

Notional costs and contingent costs: what are they?

When equalizing the value of your assets and debts, they should be reduced for the eventual costs associated with their disposition, including any taxes. They are called "notional" or "contingent" because they will only happen upon an event taking place in the future. These notional costs are relevant to ensure that equalization is based on everything at its lowest common denominator, which is an after-tax-and-costs value.

For example, $10,000 in a bank account doesn't have any costs if you were to withdraw it, but a $10,000 RRSP would require you to pay income tax when withdrawn. The amount of tax will depend on your income tax bracket at the time of withdrawal. For the equalization calculation, you would need to predict the date you would withdraw your RRSP, what the present value of your tax bracket would be at that time, and deduct that estimated tax from the value of the RRSP.

The most common notional or contingent costs are realtor fees on real estate property, taxes on retirement assets and any unrealized capital gains or losses on taxable capital assets. Taxable capital assets typically include non-registered investment accounts and any real estate that does not qualify for what is called the "Principal Residence Exemption." There are others, but these are the most common.

With assets that will attract tax based upon some future event, you must consider those tax consequences, so that equalization is equitable and someone is not surprised by having to pay unexpected tax in the future.

THE MATRIMONIAL HOME

If one of us wants to buy the family home, how do we decide what it's worth?

If you and your spouse cannot agree on one of you buying out the other's interest, the house will need to be sold. If one of you wants to buy the other's interest in the family home, you will need to agree on a value. Aside from selling it on the open market, there is no perfect method. The following are some of the more commonly discussed options:

1. **Real Estate Agent Opinion** - This is a very common approach. Often, two or three agents are asked to provide an opinion of value

on the house. This is an opinion of what the house would sell for rather than what they would list for. There may or may not be a cost charged by the agent. It is best if these agents have an arm's-length relationship, meaning that they do not have a connection to one spouse or the other.

2. **Appraisals** – You could hire a professional appraiser to value your property. There will be a cost for this service, and it often includes information on comparative sales in the neighbourhood. It may or may not be more accurate than the real estate agent opinion.

3. **Bank Appraisal** – Banks can fund up to 80 percent of the value of your home in a conventional mortgage and their appraisals may build a safety factor into the value to account for any market decreases. Also, their appraisal may only reflect a value that the property must meet in order to provide the mortgage or line-of-credit limit that you have requested. For example, if you require a line of credit or mortgage for $500,000 and your house is worth $1,000,000, the bank valuation may come back with a value that exceeds that financing limit but may not accurately reflect the actual value.

4. **Municipal Property Assessment (MPAC in Ontario)** – These values are used for the purposes of assessing a rate for property taxes. The value should be in line with the values of other homes in the neighbourhood, which makes it fair for its purpose of calculating property tax, but it is very unlikely that the home value reflects the fair market value of your individual property. This is not a good option for determining fair market value.

When you sell the home to your former partner there will be no real estate fees at that time. Instead, the fees are being deferred and the person buying the interest will need to pay them in the future. This delay of an expense is called a "notional or contingent cost."

The law cannot force either one of you to sell to the other and can only order the house to be sold.

What is our furniture and other stuff worth?

Our household possessions are valuable to us for many reasons, but the reality is that our furniture and personal belongings have very little monetary value. The law values it on resale, generally garage-sale, value rather than replacement value or original cost.

So how can you divide your personal possessions in a way that feels okay to you and your spouse?

One idea is for both of you to make a list of what you want, and each gets any item on their list that is not duplicated. Then, through a coin toss to see who goes first, you will each alternate until all the items are gone.

If one person is staying in the home, they may end up keeping much or all the household furniture. In that case, some value may be assigned to help compensate the other person for new items.

For smaller things like kitchen items and linens, you or your former partner could divide everything into two piles and the other can have first pick.

PENSIONS

What happens with my pension?

There are two kinds of pensions. One is a "Defined Contribution Pension Plan" (DCPP) and the other is a "Defined Benefit Pension Plan" (DBPP).

A DCPP is just like an RRSP except that there are limitations around access to the funds. For the purposes of property valuation, the statement value for a DCPP on the date of separation is the value for family law purposes. If you agree to transfer any funds to your partner, you will have to go through a formal process of valuation, but the value will be the same as the statement value.

The DBPP is entirely different from any other asset that we commonly see on a property statement. This type of plan typically provides an income stream to the plan member or pensioner for the entire period of retirement. If the pensioner has a spouse and the pension plan allows for a survivor benefit, the pension will pay their surviving spouse a pension when the pensioner dies, typically at 50–60 percent of the full benefit for the remainder of their life.

The DBPP must be valued for family law which is basically the present value of the future income stream using prescribed assumptions.

Defined Benefit Pensions must be valued for family law purposes. Contact your company's pension administrator to find out if they will do the valuation, how much they charge, and how long it will take.

Do I have to give half of my pension to my spouse?

People with pensions are often very protective of this asset, more so than other assets. They are often relieved to hear that they are not obligated to transfer any part of that pension to their spouse. Instead, they have an obligation to share the *value* of the pension. The options for doing so can depend on whether it is a provincial or federal pension, and whether the member has begun collecting the pension as of the date of separation. Some options are:

1. **Include pension in net family property and equalize using other property**
    This would mean that the plan member keeps the pension intact and instead transfers some other asset(s) or pays a cash settlement to their former partner. This scenario allows the plan member to draw 100 percent of their pension when they retire. Generally, this option is available whether the pensioner is retired and collecting or still working.

2. **Transfer up to half of the family law value to the other spouse**
    Unless the non-member has another pension that is willing to take on the management of these additional funds, the recipient spouse will need to transfer these funds into a Locked-In Retirement Account (LIRA). A LIRA is much like an RRSP, except that there are rules about when you can start withdrawing the funds and maximums that you can withdraw each year. If you are the recipient of the LIRA, you will then have to manage the investment or hire an investment manager to do it for you, and this will entail fees. The biggest drawback is that the funds that are transferred

to the LIRA no longer guarantee a certain income for life. This guaranteed income level and the paying-for-life component is one of the biggest benefits associated with a defined benefit pension.

3. **An if-and-when scenario**

In this scenario, where the pension is not "in pay" (meaning the plan member is not already collecting a retirement income), the monthly benefit is shared between the spouses in the future when the pension begins. There may be risks to this approach, depending on the situation.

If the pension is in pay, the options might be the same as 1 and 2 above, or there may be opportunity to have a portion of the monthly pension paid directly to the non-member spouse. If the non-member spouse was named as the survivor beneficiary at the time the member began to collect, they generally cannot be removed as the beneficiary unless they agree to be. In the case of a survivor beneficiary, the valuation will include a calculation for the survivor pension and this number will be included in the assets of the non-member spouse.

PRIVATELY OWNED BUSINESS

There are several types of businesses, ranging from sole proprietorships, partnerships, and various types of corporations. Generally, the business is property whose value is equalized, and it is also a source of income which will be considered in any calculations for child and spousal support.

I have a business and I've been told it may need to be valued. Is this true, and if so, how do I do it?

Your lawyer and financial professional will be asking for financial statements and tax returns related to the business and they will want to understand many details about it. Your lawyer will talk to you about the merits of having a Chartered Business Valuator (CBV) to value the business. The cost will vary widely depending on the type of business.

What happens with the business we own together?

If you are going to continue to own the business together, then a valuation may not be necessary. Many separating people would not wish to continue to jointly own a business, therefore, unless you agree to sell the business, one person would have to buy out the other's interest, which would likely entail a business valuation.

The value of the business is equal to the home, so should we each keep one?

This may be a great solution to address your individual goals and interests and it will be something that your professional team will help you assess as you move on to looking at options.

There can be many things to consider when there is a family-owned business, from valuation to income as well as the possible effect of "double-dipping" when it comes to these two concepts. Double-dipping is when one person benefits from the value of an equalized property owned by the other person and then again when receiving support on the income that property generates. Businesses whose values make up most of the family wealth, or where both spouses are working in the business (or are joint owners), can introduce some challenges.

Some businesses will have value for family law property division while others may not.

SECTION 3

PROCESS OPTIONS

Process Choice is about the approach or method that you and your former partner use to reach agreements. Some processes allow you to be very much involved throughout the negotiation and often lead to a settlement that is more oriented toward the unique goals of you and your family. Others will have the lawyers negotiating on your behalf and, at the extreme end, will involve a judge making the decision.

CREATING A SEPARATION AGREEMENT

What is the process for figuring this all out?

There are several ways for you and your spouse to have the conversations needed to sort these issues out. Most people can figure things out with the right support, and this guide is primarily intended as a resource for people trying to reach an agreement out of court.

There are basically four options for reaching an agreement and all are described in more detail later. **Mediation** is an option where one person is hired by both you and your spouse to facilitate the discussions between you until an agreement is reached. **Collaborative practice** is where each person hires a specially trained lawyer, and you, your former partner, and each of your collaborative lawyers work together to reach an agreement. Most often in collaborative practice there is also at least one jointly retained person, who could be either a financial professional or a family/parenting professional. The third option is a **regular negotiation**, with each of you and your spouse hiring lawyers to try to reach a resolution. And finally, there is the **do-it-yourself approach**, where you and your partner do most of the discussions and negotiations on your own.

The three authors work mostly in collaborative practice and mediation, and believe that these two options meet the needs of most separating people.

What's special about collaborative practice and mediation?

Collaborative practice and mediation are both structured settlement processes in which the goals and concerns that matter most to each person are considered in addition to legal rights and responsibilities. This is sometimes called "interest-based negotiation," and it is a problem-solving approach to conflict that focuses on needs, desires, concerns, and fears rather than just legal entitlements.

When negotiations focus solely on legal entitlements, they tend to lead to win-lose outcomes, where one person wins and gets what they want and the other person loses and does not get what they want.

When negotiations factor in both legal entitlements and the concerns that really matter to each person, they often lead to win-win outcomes, where each person's needs and concerns are addressed as best as possible.

What else do I need to know about collaborative practice?

In collaborative practice, you and your spouse will each have your own lawyer, and in many cases you will share a financial professional and a family professional. In this way, the legal issues will be addressed with each of you having the support of your respective lawyer. The financial issues will be addressed both with the support of your respective lawyers and that of a jointly retained financial professional. The parenting issues will be addressed with the support of the jointly retained family professional and your respective lawyers as needed.

The collaborative lawyers, financial professionals, and family professionals have all been trained in collaborative practice, negotiation and communication. In collaborative practice, the team works with an "interest-based approach," meaning they will ask questions to understand the most important goals and concerns for you and your spouse.

Your lawyer will be with you every step of the way, and is committed to helping you reach an out-of-court settlement that meets your most important goals and addresses your biggest concerns.

One of the key components of collaborative practice is that neither of the collaborative lawyers (or other team members) are permitted to represent you or your former partner in litigation if the attempt at a collaborative resolution fails. This is a key element of the collaborative process: it keeps both you and the lawyers focused entirely on settlement and allows you to have safe conversations that will not be used against you later.

In collaborative practice, you, your spouse, and both lawyers work through the issues together. This can often be undertaken in the same room, either with the whole team or select professionals only, depending on the issues being discussed.

Your financial professional (financial planner, accountant, or valuator) will streamline the gathering and analysis of financial documentation. They also add value to brainstorming sessions at which options are generated.

Your family professionals (parenting mediators, neutral facilitators, coaches, or child specialists) will provide a wealth of information and support to ensure that your children are protected from conflict and assisted with their transition to the new family structure. They also help the process run smoothly by facilitating meetings and helping communications move forward.

This sounds expensive . . . is it?

Collaborative practice is designed to assign the most qualified person to a task, so it is more about redistributing the same work that needs to be done to different team members as opposed to adding more work. For example, it makes sense for a family professional to work with you and your partner on parenting issues rather than two lawyers assisting you. The family professional has more expertise on parenting issues and is less expensive than the two lawyers.

What is mediation?

In mediation, you and your spouse work with a jointly retained mediator who will help you and your former partner discuss and negotiate the issues. Much like collaborative-practice professionals, mediators typically work with an interest-based approach, eliciting the most important goals and concerns for you and your partner.

Most often in mediation, you and your former partner will work directly with the mediator in three-way meetings without lawyers, although sometimes the lawyers may also be present. Prior to signing the separation agreement, each spouse needs to have his or her own lawyer review the draft agreement.

This is called "independent legal advice." It is best to obtain independent legal advice early and throughout the mediation process.

Co-mediation also allows for the integrated involvement of financial professionals and family professionals. In co-mediation, a family professional and a lawyer might co-mediate the issues with the family professional mediator working mostly on the parenting issues, and the lawyer mediator working mostly on the financial issues. Co-mediation may also involve a lawyer and financial professional working together on all legal and financial issues. A third co-mediation combination may involve a family professional and a financial professional working on issues together.

What else do I need to know before I pick mediation?

The mediator does not make any decisions for either party, they simply facilitate the negotiation process.

There will be an intake process where you may be asked to complete a questionnaire, and you will likely have an individual intake meeting with the mediator before you and your spouse meet with the mediator together. This is also an opportunity for you, your spouse, and the mediator to decide if mediation is a good fit.

While the role of the mediator is to help you speak and be heard—and listen and understand your spouse—mediation requires that you feel somewhat comfortable and empowered to speak for yourself. If you are in mediation without lawyers present, you will be expected to negotiate for yourself while the mediator facilitates the negotiation.

Finally, there are two kinds of mediation, open and closed. Closed mediation means that if the process breaks down, you agree that information from the process cannot be used in other legal proceedings, and that you agree not to subpoena the mediator, although it is a judge's prerogative to do so. Open mediation means that the issues discussed between yourself and your mediator, along with their notes, can be used in another process and that the mediator can be subpoenaed by you.

What's the same about mediation and collaborative practice?

Mediation and collaborative practice are both interest-based processes. This means that, while the law is still relevant, the goals and concerns that really matter to you and your spouse form the basis for the conversation and negotiation rather than just focusing on legal rights and entitlements.

What is the difference between mediation and collaborative practice?

One difference between mediation and collaborative practice is that the lawyers involved in collaborative practice have been trained in negotiation theory and practice, family systems, problem solving, communication, and conflict resolution. The lawyers supporting you in mediation may not have this additional training.

Another difference is that the lawyers provide advocacy throughout the entire process, whereas in mediation the lawyers typically play a smaller role toward the end of the process.

Finally, collaborative practice requires each of you to promise to hire new lawyers if the process fails to produce an agreement and you wish to go to court. In mediation your lawyer can continue to represent you if the mediation is unsuccessful and you need to go to court.

Collaborative practice has more structured process protocols in place because of the integrated team of legal, financial, and family professionals.

Mediation and collaborative practice can have a great deal of overlap but are distinct processes. Selecting the process that best suits your unique circumstance can help increase your satisfaction with the result of the process.

What is traditional negotiation?

In a typical negotiation, you and your spouse each retain your own lawyer. The first step is often the exchange of financial documentation. The negotiation process is not structured or consistent. Usually, the lawyers then exchange settlement proposals and counterproposals. Once the issues are narrowed, there is sometimes a four-way settlement meeting (both lawyers and both clients). If someone is not getting what they want, there is often a threat that they will start a court proceeding. Often the parenting issues are mediated by a parenting mediator while the financial issues are negotiated through the lawyers.

What is litigation and arbitration?

When a couple is unable to reach agreement on one or more issues, it may be necessary to have a court or arbitrator decide.

Most family courts are case-managed and designed to encourage early settlement. In Ontario, the first stage of a court proceeding is a "case conference," in which the court ensures that financial disclosure is being exchanged. The case conference is followed by a settlement conference, in which the judge attempts to assist the couple in settling the issues in dispute. Most cases result in settlement but it can be a long process. Very few cases proceed all the way to trial.

Arbitration is like litigation, except that the person making the decision is an experienced family lawyer who is jointly selected, hired, and paid for by the spouses.

What if we want to do it ourselves?

Some couples can discuss and negotiate issues directly between themselves. These discussions are sometimes called "kitchen table negotiations."

It is often very difficult to stand up for yourself in the weeks or months following a separation, because you may be feeling sad, exhausted, and vulnerable. It is hard to take a businesslike approach to financial issues when you are experiencing intense emotions. Having a professional support you in the negotiations will help you separate emotions from other issues and will help you navigate the challenging path of deciding what you might need to let go of versus what you need to advocate strongly for.

In addition, there are many settlement opportunities that can have a positive financial impact on your future, and involving the right professionals can help ensure that you take advantage of them wherever appropriate. Since these opportunities may be unique to the area of separation, it is best to involve professionals who specialize in the field. Your settlement has the potential to impact you and your children for the balance of your life, and utilizing divorce professionals can help to ensure you make fully informed decisions.

Although some people can work things out on their own, it is better suited for those who have not been together for a long time, have very little property, and no dependent children. And no matter what, it is still important for each to retain a lawyer for independent legal advice.

Which process is right for me?

If you think that you and your former partner have a good chance of negotiating in a room with just the two of you and the mediator, mediation may be a good, cost-effective fit. One of the benefits of mediation is the simplicity of the model, with the work being done in a centralized way through the mediator.

If you or your former partner are worried about being able to speak up for yourselves or there is a power imbalance around information or negotiation, the extra support of your lawyer in collaborative practice may be a better fit. Also, if you think the extra support in preparing for meetings and making decisions would be helpful, then collaborative practice may be a better decision than mediation. If you think that the added skills and knowledge of the family and financial professionals would be helpful, collaborative practice is advised. One of the benefits of the collaborative-practice model is the integration of legal, financial, and family professionals.

I have chosen the process, what's next?

Any of the out-of-court options require both you and your former partner to agree to that approach. So, the first step is to introduce your former partner to the process you would like. This may mean sending them to a provincial website for mediation or collaborative practice. It may mean telling them what you have learned about the options. Many divorce professionals who work in collaborative practice or mediation will spend some time with you talking about the different process options without charging a fee.

Once your partner agrees to one of these options, the next step is to hire your team. The section titled, "The Professionals," has some tips on how to choose the right team members.

What do I need to do to be prepared?

- Think through the things that matter most to you and start to prioritize them.
- Begin to gather your financial information.
- Open a digital or paper folder to keep your questions and notes all in one place.

There will be a lot of information coming your way, so you may want to take notes during your preparation meetings with your divorce professionals, or even bring a trusted friend or family member along. Reviewing your notes afterward and noting any questions or clarifications will allow you to have a focused follow-up call or email with your lawyer, family professional, or financial professional.

How can I negotiate a good deal for myself?

First and foremost, you need to develop a sense of what you want and need, and why. And you need to start to prioritize the things that matter most to you.

You need to think of negotiation as a partnership of both sides of the negotiation table. For this to work, you need to listen with curiosity to your former partner and their lawyer—and they need to see that you are doing so. Curious listening does *not* mean agreeing with the other, it means acknowledging and understanding their point of view. It means that instead of thinking up retorts while they are talking, you are listening with full attention and focusing on understanding their perspective. You also need to say what matters to you in a way that can be heard by your former partner.

Negotiations involve trades, gives, takes, and compromises. There is a time and a place for each. The better you understand what you want and need and what your former partner wants and needs, the better you will be able to make decisions on when to stand firm and when to let go.

Why wouldn't I want what the law says I'm entitled to?

In a divorce, it is important to know what a court might say about your situation so that you can make fully informed decisions. Courts, however, are bound by law to apply a cookie-cutter approach to many legal issues, as they must apply a default set of principles. The truth is, however, that each separating family is unique. Given this uniqueness, the more open you and your spouse are to solutions that might be different from what a court would say, the more successful the negotiation may be. Sometimes that may mean getting what you would be entitled to, but getting it in a different form or method.

How do I know when to settle?

Knowing when to settle may be a gradual process, or it may hit you in an obvious *a-ha* moment. If the feeling of being ready to settle lasts for a few days in a row, it's a good sign that you are feeling prepared to do so. If you can detail the pros and cons to someone close to you and explain clearly how you have come to your decision to settle, this likely indicates that you're ready to move on.

It is helpful to imagine yourself three years in the future and settled along the lines you are thinking of, and picture how you will feel. It is easy to give in, give up, and settle in an unsatisfactory way because you just want to get things over with, and the three-year check-in exercise can help you avoid that. It is also easy to get stuck and draw lines in the sand, and this check-in can help make sure the process is not getting mired in something that in the long run won't make a lot of difference to you.

I want peace, but at what cost?

You may worry that you have to give in on everything that matters just to keep the peace. It is understandable if you have such fears, and attaining peace is hard work, but it is a realistic goal that does not require complete acquiescence.

The first step in handling tough decisions is to stop thinking about whether you want to give in to your spouse. Instead, focus on the ways you and those closest to you will be impacted by your decision.

Stay focused on the big picture. Does this issue significantly impact one of your most important hopes and/or fears around separation? Ask yourself whether deep down you believe this issue will matter in your everyday life one year, or even five years, from today.

A key ingredient in making a decision you can live with is having a realistic picture of your alternatives to settlement. Making sense of whether to continue negotiations depends in part on the best and worst-case scenarios that would happen if you gave up negotiating. You need to be realistic about this. With an overly optimistic picture, you might end negotiations prematurely. With an overly pessimistic picture, you might continue even when it would make better sense to end them.

It is important to bear in mind not just what the outcome might look like in a non-negotiation process, such as court or arbitration, but also the implications for your emotions, finances, relationships, and time.

If you keep these ideas in mind when a tough decision comes up, you will be better equipped to make the decision that works best for you and your family.

SECTION 4

THE PROFESSIONALS

Hiring a lawyer is what many people will initially think about when they separate but the reality is that a separation is more than just a legal transaction. There are many financial issues to be resolved and many decisions to be made about your children and, while your lawyer may be able to assist you in all areas, they may not be your best resource for a particular task.

There are other professionals working in separation that can also help you navigate the path to reach a successful agreement with your former partner. Used as a resource to complement the services of your lawyer, these professionals can help to ensure that your agreement meets the unique needs of you and your family.

THE LAWYER

Why do I need a lawyer?

Family law is complicated and the decisions you make now will impact you, your family, and your finances for a long time. A lawyer will ensure that you understand your legal rights and responsibilities and help you evaluate settlement options in the context of those rights and responsibilities. A lawyer will help you "think through your thinking," when it comes time to making decisions. Further, a collaborative lawyer will support you and be your advocate along the way. Sometimes that will mean helping you assert yourself and sometimes it will mean providing a reality check on whether your expectations are reasonably attainable.

While cost is always a concern, keep in mind that you are making major decisions that will impact your life.

What should I think about when hiring a lawyer?

Some things to consider when hiring a lawyer are how much family law experience the lawyer has, and whether it is an interest-based process such as collaborative practice or mediation.

Other important factors are their hourly rate and their availability to take you on as a client to give you the timely attention you need.

It is helpful to ask the lawyer about their views on overcoming negotiation challenges, typical time and cost of their cases, tips on keeping costs down, expectations of you as a client, and your lawyer's relationship and history with your spouse's lawyer.

There is no harm in interviewing a few lawyers to get a sense of their personalities and what each has to offer. Some lawyers can be more litigious in their perspective and approach, while others are trained to be more collaborative. Choose a lawyer whose philosophy is more in keeping with your own approach and outlook, and one you feel will be able to help you achieve an outcome that addresses most of your important goals and concerns.

You will work very closely with your lawyer throughout your divorce process, and a good fit will allow you to feel informed and supported along the way.

When should I retain a lawyer?

The earlier the better. There are some decisions that you may need to make early on that could have long-term impact. It is best to have relevant information before moving out, putting the house up for sale, or making early temporary parenting or financial agreements. A lawyer is also an important person to discuss your process options with before choosing mediation or collaborative practice.

How do I find a lawyer?

Referrals from friends or family members who had positive experiences with their lawyer are a good place to start, especially if those experiences were in a settlement process like mediation or collaborative practice. You can also look at a local collaborative divorce website. There is one provincial group for all the collaborative professionals in Ontario and their website has helpful information on how to find a lawyer. If you are already working with a family or financial professional, they may also be able to provide you with referrals.

THE FAMILY PROFESSIONAL, THERAPIST and PARENTING MEDIATOR

Why do I need a family professional, therapist or parenting mediator?

A family professional, therapist or parenting mediator is often a Registered Social Worker who will typically have their Master of Social Work (MSW), a Registered Psychologist who will hold a doctoral degree (PHD), a Registered Psychotherapist or an Accredited Family Mediator. These professionals may be an integral part of your mediation or collaborative team or they may offer support outside of the mediation or collaborative process.

Let's first distinguish between the different types of professionals:

Qualified **therapists** who are experienced in separation and divorce can work with you individually outside of the collaborative process and provide you with emotional support and guidance. If needed, one or both of you can hire separate therapists to support each of you individually as you move forward in your process.

A **parenting mediator** is a neutral person who will work with both of you to help you create a parenting plan, and facilitate any difficult conversations you and your former partner may wish or need to have.

A **family professional** is someone working within the collaborative process in a neutral role to support and help both separating partners. The family professional may help clarify concerns, manage emotions, and also help members of the collaborative team communicate more effectively and stay productive and resolution focused.

The above professionals can make a difference to you and your process. When there is a high degree of conflict, or where you or your partner are experiencing mental health or addiction challenges, a family professional or therapist is even more important. After all, this is an emotionally trying time in your life. This, coupled with navigating your way through financial negotiations and the complexities of the law, can often become overwhelming. In addition, disputes over parenting time and parental decisions can become highly emotional. In court, couples can spend large amounts of money on endless battles related to parenting time. Such battles can impact both parents' ability to care for the children.

A parenting mediator or a collaboratively trained family professional can play a key role in working with parents to provide a much-needed source of objectivity and balance, rather than letting their emotions become a (hidden) barrier to settlement. While the lawyers can also provide some help related to emotional concerns, the lawyer's role is primarily to address legal matters.

Family professionals and parenting mediators can also help if there has been violence or abuse in the relationship. These professionals can work with one or both of you to ensure that you are listened to and understood, and to make sure that you have a safe space to articulate your concerns and needs. They can help ensure that both of you feel confident enough to negotiate and also support you in keeping the past from preventing you from fully participating in the divorce process. The main challenge in these situations is when a power imbalance prevents meaningful negotiations between former partners.

Sometimes a history of abuse or violence makes collaborative practice or mediation inappropriate altogether. At other times, the combination of a lawyer advocating for each spouse within a collaborative process, combined with the help of a neutral family professional, may help overcome the challenges and reach a settlement.

In collaborative practice today, family professionals can be key members of the team. The value of family professionals working within a collaborative team is that they are working for both of you and they help things from becoming too adversarial. Additionally, they are trained to be knowledgeable and sensitive to emotional issues. Based on discussions with you, your spouse, and the children, they can provide neutral and objective information on hot-button parenting issues. This approach is very different than traditional family law settlements that are mostly done through back and forth letters between the lawyers.

This is an emotional process, and having a neutral professional to support you and help you navigate your way through, while also considering your children's needs, can be an invaluable asset.

What should I think about when hiring a family professional, therapist or parenting mediator?

Your therapist, family professional or parenting mediator should ideally have specialized experience and knowledge in separation and divorce. Their experience in this area, coupled with their understanding of relationship dynamics, will allow them to help you understand and assess your children's needs as well as your own barriers to resolution. You should feel that the professional you are working with is acting as a neutral party, with no investment in the outcome of your agreements. In general, regardless of which professional you hire, having a good rapport with and confidence in any professional you work with is critical. You will want to feel comfortable in your interactions with them, so that you can speak your mind with ease. Here are some specifics points of consideration for each type of professional:

Therapist: If you are seeking the services of a therapist to work with you individually, ensure that they are knowledgeable about separation and the types of concerns that typically arise. Be sure to ask about their fees and availability. Meet with the therapist for an initial session before committing yourself to them, in order to make sure you are feeling comfortable and are connecting with them.

Parenting Mediator: Ensure that the professional you are working with has a solid understanding of separation and divorce related issues. It can be helpful to ask if they generally conduct mediation with or without the clients' lawyers needing to be present. Ask them if they offer closed or open mediation. Closed mediation means that if the process breaks down, you agree not to use the mediator's notes in a different process, and open mediation means that you can use the mediator's notes in another process. Find out about their fees and availability. Most importantly, you want to feel like the meditator hears you and understands you.

Family Professional: You will want to ensure that your family professional is collaboratively trained and a member of the collaborative practice community they belong to, which will mean that they are also part of a regulatory body. Ask what the hourly rate of the family professional is and whether they require a retainer (money up front). You will also want to know what their availability is for working with you.

Make sure you work with a professional who has appropriate credentials and with whom you feel comfortable.

How do I find a family professional, therapist, or parenting mediator?

Refer to your local collaborative practice group's website in order to gain a better understanding of what collaborative practice offers, as well as names of family professionals. In Ontario that is the Ontario Association of Collaborative Professionals website (www.oacp.co).

To find an accredited family mediator for the parenting issues, you may refer to your local family mediation website. In Ontario that is either the Ontario Association for Family Mediation (OAFM) (www.oafm.on.ca) or the Family Dispute Resolution Institute of Ontario (FIDRIO) (www.fdrio.ca)

To find a therapist in Canada, you can go to www.findasocialworker.ca or www.findapsychologist.ca. You can also internet search Find A Professional - OAMHP (Ontario Association of Mental Health Professionals). In general, the region you live in will likely have community resources that may be government funded or offer services on a sliding fee scale. If the agency has a waiting list and you are eager to find more immediate aid, you can ask them for referrals. You can also ask your family doctor, friends, lawyer, or financial professional for referrals.

THE FINANCIAL PROFESSIONAL

Why and when do I need a financial professional?

Financial professionals can be key members of your team. They help to "grow the pie" in a way that ensures the pieces are bigger when sliced up, in a sensible, durable, and tax-efficient way. The financial professional can get involved in any aspect of the separation as it relates to your finances and become involved at any time in the process. It is often ideal if they are involved right at the beginning.

What does a financial professional do?

A financial professional can help you divide your property and deal with child and spousal support in a manner that will ensure that it maximizes social benefits, minimizes taxes, and takes advantages of unique opportunities that may not have been available to you in the past. Certified Financial Planners (CFP) have expertise in personal finances, including tax strategy, money management and lifestyle spending, estate and retirement planning, as well as risk management. A CFP who has specialized training in divorce finances may be able to help you and your spouse achieve some creative solutions. Sometimes the money-saving opportunities your financial professional suggests can entirely offset their fees, and if they are working to establish child or spousal support, which can be a significant part of the process, the fees related to those activities are generally tax-deductible to the recipient of support.

Often, you and your former partner won't have equal knowledge or understanding of the family's finances, or finances in general. Even where the knowledge is similar, emotional issues can interfere with the ability to understand all the information and to make good, durable decisions. This can lead to a longer process and drive costs up for both people. Ultimately you have a shared goal to get through the process in an effective, timely, and cost-efficient manner, and the financial professional can help you do this by spending whatever time it takes to get you to a place where you can confidently make decisions.

Here are some of the tasks that the financial professional may execute:

1. Preparing the financial documents for property equalization and making sure that everyone completely understands the information.

2. Helping to determine what income is considered for support calculations, and working with proprietary software to illustrate

various support options. They work to optimize opportunities that will provide more net disposable income in each of your homes.

3. Assisting with details around sharing of your children's extraordinary, extracurricular, and day-to-day expenses.

4. Helping you identify future lifestyle spending needs to assess your settlement options and plan accordingly.

5. Providing ideas and support in generating and assessing settlement options, and helping to explore the what-ifs.

6. Providing transitional support in implementing the separation agreements.

Even if you are not one of the many families living beyond their means before the separation, running two households on the same income(s) can be a difficult math problem to solve. While there can be additional funds that come about due to the separation, they usually do not cover the extra costs and you may need some help to figure out how to bridge the gap. A financial professional can help you develop a lifestyle spending plan and a plan for managing it with available cash flow and resources.

When a financial professional is hired to assist with understanding the value of a privately owned business, it will often be a Chartered Business Valuator (CBV). Instead of you and your spouse each hiring experts to battle it out, a jointly retained neutral valuator is usually the cost effective and efficient route to a settlement.

The involvement of a financial professional can help you keep your divorce costs down while making sure you have all the information and support you need to make good financial decisions. With lives busier than ever, families often have a divide-and-conquer approach to tasks, with the finances falling to one spouse, leaving the other in a place where they need to catch up in order to make good decisions.

Why don't I have my lawyer do it all for me?

Not every case needs a financial professional, but it is likely that all could benefit from one. There are several reasons why you may want to have a financial specialist working with you and your lawyer:

1. Cost is the first reason to consider. The financial person is working with both spouses and therefore their fee is shared between the two, which is less expensive than both lawyers doing the work.
2. The financial divorce specialist brings an expertise that the legal professional may not have.
3. Both you and your spouse will need to retain your own lawyer, but a financial divorce specialist can work with both of you. They will do some of the tasks that would otherwise be done by your lawyers' individual offices. This redundancy and duplication of efforts can be eliminated, leading to greater efficiency and cost savings.

A professional interdisciplinary team puts the right professional (legal, family, or financial) on the right task, and helps to ensure a settlement that is efficient, cost-effective, and thorough.

Why not use the accountant or financial advisor we already have?

While it is true that the professionals who are currently involved in your affairs likely have intricate knowledge of your present financial situation, using them in this process may not save you the fees that you think it might. This is not to say that your accountant or financial advisor are not valuable resources for your divorce as you work toward your agreement, but their role is much different than the divorce specialist.

The financial planners and business valuators who specialize in the areas related to family law bring a unique skillset not found in the typical financial professionals who focus on wealth management, or the accountant who focuses on your business or taxes.

Typically, your wealth advisor is compensated based on the value of the assets that you have invested with them, or the products that you purchase from them; life insurance is one common example. Their focus is largely about growing your wealth, and this also has the direct benefit of growing theirs at the same time. There is nothing wrong with this relationship, since everyone is entitled to receive compensation for their services. However, your goals when going through separation are often dramatically different then your goals when dealing with your wealth advisor. The common goal of these two financial specialists is to make sure you preserve and capitalize on as much wealth as possible, but the best solution in a separation may run counter to the interests of the investment advisor. We are not suggesting that you cannot get great honest information from your current financial people but we feel it is best to use a financial professional whose neutrality is not questioned in the future if outcomes do not match expectations.

The financial divorce professional is paid on a fee-for-service basis, and their involvement with you should come to an end when your separation agreement is complete. Any future dealings should only be under the umbrella of the separation and should not involve dealings outside of this scope. This ensures that any advice offered during the negotiation is free from conflict of interest.

A financial professional working strictly with separating couples is familiar with the legal financial documents and protocols in family law and can produce the statements very efficiently. They will use forms that allow your lawyers to work seamlessly without having to redo anything to fit their legal world. Thorough knowledge and expertise help them maximize the use of the third-party software used for calculating support scenarios.

Canada Revenue Agency (CRA) offers couples going through marital breakdown many unique opportunities with respect to redistributing their property and incomes. There are several tax credits that can have substantial financial benefits that are otherwise unavailable to intact couples. Financial specialists in separation and divorce often work in this field every day, stay current on the ever-changing rules, and can identify opportunities and implications that may not be obvious to your wealth advisor or accountant.

Bringing your own financial person into this process could put both of you in uncomfortable situations. They may have divided loyalties or be unconsciously aligned to one person due to the nature in which they are or have been involved with your family.

A financial professional specializing in separation and divorce brings a unique skillset to the process that your accountant or wealth advisor may not have. Using a financial professional who will have no future dealings with either of you ensures all information is without conflict of interest.

What should I think about when hiring a financial professional?

Sometimes financial professionals in divorce are only educated in divorce finance rather than broad-based financial planning, and this may be all you need. If your assets and debts are more complicated, you may want a financial professional with more in depth training in personal finances, such as a Certified Financial Planner (CFP), or Chartered Professional Accountant (CPA). If you are a business owner, you probably require the services of a Chartered Business Valuator (CBV).

You should ensure that whomever you choose has access to and is familiar with all the legal financial documents, so any work product can be seamlessly adopted by your lawyer. When their work is done in another format, your lawyer must familiarize themselves with this new approach and spend time putting it into the legal documentation that will be part of the separation agreement. This will add to your costs.

If a financial professional asks about your financial net worth, or suggests that you invest in a product before understanding you and your goals, they are likely not a good fit for your separation. While assets and debts are key components of separation work, they come second to understanding you and your needs at this stage. Of course, if there is a unique component to your financial makeup, you will want to find out if that financial person has experience in dealing with that type of situation before engaging their services.

If they are not going to charge you for their services, then you need to understand how they expect to be compensated for working with you. If they expect to invest your money or sell you products, they have a vested interest in finding a settlement that will produce that outcome. This situation can result in a conflict of interest and may not produce a settlement to your best advantage.

It can be helpful if your financial professional has training in family mediation. This is not an absolute must, but this skillset helps the financial professional work more efficiently with you and your former partner.

How do I find a financial professional?

In Canada, the Academy of Financial Divorce Specialists (www.afds.ca) is a source for financial divorce professionals with a variety of financial backgrounds. Membership is limited to those who hold a higher level of financial accreditation, such as a Chartered Professional Accountant (CPA) or a Certified Financial Planner (CFP), as well as a variety of other designations. Regardless of which designation, if you have any unique circumstances be sure to ask any potential professional if they have training in that specific area.

There are many collaborative practice groups throughout Ontario and Canada who will have financial professionals in their membership. The

Ontario Association of Collaborative Professionals (www.oacp.co) is a good source and has developed a certification process for all three professional groups, and anyone with the designation as an Advanced Collaborative Professional (ACP) has successfully met this high standard.

Of course, one of your other professionals may be able to suggest a financial person that would be the right fit for you.

THE MEDIATOR

How do I choose a mediator?

Let's first discuss the fact that there can be different kinds of mediators. As mentioned earlier in this guide, there are mediators who are lawyers, financial professionals, or family professionals.

Lawyer mediators tend to do comprehensive mediations, meaning they mediate parenting and financial issues, or they will mediate just the financial issues. Financial mediators tend to only mediate financial issues. Parenting mediators tend to only mediate parenting issues. Co-mediation may involve any combination of these three types of mediators.

If you would like to work with a mediator who is a lawyer, you and your former partner would jointly retain that mediator to work with both of you to help resolve the issues that you agree to mediate. The mediation contract should set out what issues are being mediated so everyone is on the same page. Once you have come to an agreement on the issues, the mediator will prepare a summary of the agreements in a document called a "Memorandum of Understanding." You will then each need to obtain independent legal advice, which means you will each need to hire your own lawyer to review the Memorandum of Understanding and confirm that you understand its consequences.

If you think a financial mediator would be the best fit, then you and your former partner will jointly hire a financial mediator who can assist you in resolving the financial issues. If an agreement is reached, the financial mediator will draft a Memorandum of Understanding for you to review with your respective lawyers.

Finally, if you are looking for a parenting mediator to support you in putting together a parenting plan, you can work with a professional who specializes in this particular area. When you have finished coming to all your agreements on the parenting issues as they relate to your children, the parenting plan will be in draft form. You will then need to review it with your lawyer.

THE COSTS

How are we going to pay for the professional fees?

The reality is that divorce is very expensive. Most people do not have extra cash available to pay the costs and must find other sources. The most common way is to access the equity in your home using a "home equity line of credit," often called a "secured line of credit." This is the least expensive option, since it usually offers funds at the lowest possible interest rate available to most people.

If you do not own a home or you cannot choose this option, then the next best choice would be to visit your bank to set up an unsecured line of credit. This will have a higher interest rate, but it is a good way to get access to fairly low-rate funds, assuming you have a decent credit rating.

Using a credit card that you are not able to pay off in full each month is a very expensive way to pay (for anything), and would not be an efficient way to fund the costs. In most cases, RRSP withdrawals are not an ideal option either, since tax will be withheld at the time of withdrawal and will often require further payment when filing your annual tax return.

How do I keep my costs down?

Mediation and collaborative practitioners make a point of working cases in an efficient and cost-effective manner. Nonetheless, professional hourly fees can add up quickly. You don't want those costs to get out of control, so here are some tips for managing the costs of your case:

1. Before phoning your lawyer or other professional, make a list of the topics you want to discuss in the conversation. Before you make the call, try to clarify your goals as much as you can.

2. Try to limit yourself to sending no more than one email per day per professional. In the course of a day, there might be any number of questions you want to ask or things you want to say, and an efficient approach is to keep an email in your draft folder that you add to throughout the day. Before sending, organize the bits of information and even try to add what you think might be the answer to some of the questions. This will give the professional the opportunity to respond in a more efficient, cost-effective, and customized way.

3. Get your homework done and send it to your lawyer or financial professional all at once rather than piecemeal, on or before the agreed-upon date. If your lawyer or financial professionals must send you reminders you may be charged for their time, and turning up for meetings without having done your assigned task(s) will result in costly and less-productive meetings. A notebook can be helpful to keep track of your to-do list.

4. Read and re-read every handout from your professionals so that they can focus on giving you customized, valuable information specific to your situation.

5. Save your settlement dollars for issues that really mean a lot to you, either financially or emotionally, and try not to sweat the small stuff. Professional time is expensive, and potential upsides of a win on a particular issue may cost you more in fees than they are actually worth. If in doubt, ask a member of your team for their thoughts on the costs versus benefits of the situation.

We know what we want the agreement to say, so why spend all this money?

There are many elements at play when a couple goes through a separation, and emotions can run high. During this time, you are negotiating financial agreements that have the potential to affect you and your children for the remainder of your life. For most, negotiating a separation agreement is not something they have ever done before and there are many issues that may get missed and many possible solutions that may not be known. The best way to ensure that it works for your family is thorough financial disclosure, using specialists who can identify the best opportunities available while avoiding potential pitfalls that may arise in the future.

Durability of the agreement can rest on financial disclosure. Disclosing all property and income sources does not mean that you must share them, and if you and your spouse agree to move away from a legal model that is your choice. What is important is knowing exactly what you have chosen to give up. Imagine how you would feel if in the future your spouse has a standard of living dramatically better than yours due to some fact that you had not known at separation, and which may have allowed you to make different choices.

It is key that you get independent legal advice to understand your rights, and full financial disclosure allows your lawyer to advise you of those rights in the context of your situation.

You may very well have an answer that you both feel works for your family, but an experienced family lawyer and a financial professional will make sure that you are aware of the many other financial settlement options that might be available that could meet your goals as well as minimize tax consequences and maximize other benefits. Full financial disclosure gives your professionals all the tools they need to do the best possible job for you.

Ensuring that your decisions are well thought out and made from a fully informed position is your best chance of moving forward without having regrets or resentment if things do not turn out as expected in the future.

SECTION 5

ADDITIONAL INFORMATION

The legal aspects of separation will have you making many decisions about dividing your assets and debts, sharing your incomes and parenting your children. There are many other financial areas that the legal process does not often address and that we commonly hear about from our clients. They include simple questions about how to file taxes in the year of separation to bigger questions about meeting the increased expenses associated with their new family structure.

TAXES AND BENEFITS

How do we file taxes this year?

The CRA does not consider you as separated until you and your spouse or common-law partner have lived in separate residences for a period of no less than 90 days. If you separated toward the end of the tax year, you should delay filing your taxes until at least 90 days after that date; for example, filing no sooner than March 15 if you separated on December 15. By doing this you can claim the tax credits that you are entitled to without having to submit an adjustment later, and it will ensure that any social benefits are started as soon as possible.

Can I expect some tax breaks and social benefits as a single parent?

Entitlement to the social benefits below are based on the income of the family, and when a couple separates, one or both parties may now be entitled to benefits they would not otherwise have received if they were still living together. This is because their family income is now based on their sole earnings, rather than the combined income of the two spouses. These benefits can help you offset some of the additional costs associated with having two residences.

1. Canada Child Benefit (CCB) is a tax-free monthly allowance for parents of children up to 18 years of age. Married and single

parents are eligible to receive this benefit, and the amount will depend on family income and the number of children. Entitlement to the benefit is automatically assessed when you file your taxes, and in order to qualify and collect, taxes must be filed every year, even if you do not have any income.

2. The GST/HST credit is a tax-free payment paid quarterly to lower-income families and individuals to help them offset all or part of the GST/HST that they pay on goods and services. You do not have to apply, since it is automatically determined during the assessment of your annual income tax filing.

3. The Eligible Dependent Credit is a non-refundable tax credit that reduces the amount of tax payable, and it is available to single and separated parents with children 18 years of age and under. In shared parenting situations where there are two or more children, both parents may be able to claim this credit. You will find forms TD1 and TD1ON (Ontario version) on line that you can submit to your payroll department to have your taxes reduced immediately.

4. Other benefits associated with your province of residence, such as the Trillium Benefit in Ontario, will be triggered through the filing of your tax return.

Filing forms to change your marital status and child residence arrangement with CRA as soon as you have physically lived separate and apart for 90 days will get social benefits into your hands as soon as possible.

HEALTH BENEFITS

Will I be able to stay on my ex-partner's health plan?

Sometimes one of you has no group health coverage because your employer does not offer a plan, or more commonly, because they have not been employed outside of the home. Provided that you are only separated as opposed to divorced, you are still considered to be a spouse, and most plans will allow a separated spouse to stay on the plan. Check with the employer or plan administrator to confirm their policies. If it is possible and this is something that you have agreed to, it should be included in the separation agreement, and it is often stated as an agreement to keep the former partner on the plan for so long as they are able. If the person with the health plan wanted to add a common-law spouse in the future, this would likely trigger a reassessment of coverage, since health plans only allow for the coverage of one spouse, even if you have not divorced.

If you are no longer able to stay insured on your former partner's plan, you may want to look into options to purchase your own health insurance. There are health insurance plans that will allow you to purchase coverage without any medical approval, but generally these need to be put into place within 30 days of being removed from any existing plan. Start with contacting the existing insurer to see what they can offer you.

HIGHER COSTS OF TWO HOMES

**How are we going to manage the additional
costs of running two homes?**

Without question, it costs more to run two households than one. While there are some tax savings to spousal support and some additional benefits available to separated spouses, it may still be necessary to find ways to reduce expenses or access additional funds. The financial specialist will work with you both to help craft a settlement and restructure your finances in a way that best addresses this challenge.

RENTING VERSUS BUYING

I really want to own a home rather than rent. How can I do that?

Decisions about whether to buy versus rent are both financial and emotional. The definition of rent is to pay someone for the use of something, and the reality is that there are many forms of rent when you buy a home. Property taxes, property insurance, and mortgage interest all fall within this definition. Homes require maintenance and upgrades if they are expected to maintain their value and stay on par with the neighbourhood. Realtor fees and land-transfer taxes are significant costs associated with sale and purchase. The reality is that home ownership is fraught with additional costs, and studies show that renters can be just as wealthy, if not wealthier, than homeowners if they take their capital and funds associated with these additional costs and invest them elsewhere.

One of the benefits of renting for a period is that it allows you to take a breath and settle into your new life. You can take your time to shop for a new home without the stress of your separation and after having had some experience with your new financial situation. Generally, renting for a period of time will not have any material effect on your long-term financial future.

If your decision is to buy a new home, you may be able to access up to $35,000 from your RRSP under the marital breakdown rules associated with the Home Buyers Plan.

Buying and selling a home is costly, with land transfer taxes on the buying end, real estate fees on the selling end, and other closing costs on both ends. It is especially important to consider how long you will want to stay in this new home before making a buying decision.

RETIREMENT

**I am worried about my retirement now that we
are separating. Will I ever be able to retire?**

Balancing day-to-day expenses and retirement savings is a challenge for
many people whether they are separating or not. Separation is a time when
you will need to re-evaluate your goals, and delayed retirement may be a
consequence. Your financial professional can work with you to understand
your goals and concerns and ultimately help you develop financial settlement
options that will address your retirement concerns, while considering any
obligations you may have.

RETRAINING - GOING BACK TO WORK

I am going to have to go back to school. How will I afford that?

If you or your former partner have RRSP funds and your program meets the criteria, you may be able to access some of these funds on a tax-free basis to help support you while attending school.

CONCLUSION

We hope that this guide is helpful to you and that you will be surrounded by a supportive professional team. While separation is one of life's most stressful events, we believe that you will find your way through in small and meaningful steps. We wish you all the best in this next chapter of your life.

ABOUT THE AUTHORS

Stella Kavoukian has a Master of Social Work and is accredited as an advanced collaborative professional. She has over 25 years of clinical experience working as a child, adult, and family therapist, and trains professionals in the area of separation and divorce. She works with parents in developing cooperative parenting plans and encouraging effective communication and resolution. Stella believes that an empathic approach allows for the building of trust and mutual respect, and that responsible, kind co-parenting is the foundation for positively supporting children when parents separate.

Alison Anderson is a Certified Financial Planner, Financial Divorce Specialist and trained family mediator. She is accredited as an advanced collaborative professional and teaches collaborative practice courses. Her practice, located in the Toronto area, has been dedicated to working with clients going through separation and divorce since 2010. The added value that she brings to the process allows clients to fully understand all aspects of their financial situation and the impact of the options available to them, and to maximize income-saving opportunities and social benefits.

Deborah Graham is a family lawyer and is accredited both as a family mediator and an advanced collaborative professional. She has over 25 years of experience working with separating and divorcing families. Deborah teaches introductory and advanced collaborative process and mediation courses and is a sought-after international trainer. She is passionate about empowering clients with legal information and negotiation coaching so they can fully participate in settlement discussions in both the collaborative process and mediation, and so that they can feel confident in making decisions as they move forward with their lives.

Illustrations by **Chloe Kavoukian-Scharf.** Chloe lives in Toronto and is an Ontario Certified Teacher for deaf and hard-of-hearing students. She enjoys incorporating art and creativity into her work and paints as a hobby.